XX 49

Five Against Pollution

Philip Hewitt

Cornelsen

Cornelsen English Library

Verlagsredaktion
Dr. Blanca-Maria Rudhart

Umschlaggestaltung
hawemannundmosch, Berlin

Titelbilder
Landschaft: Shutterstock.com/Phil Harland
Mann: Shutterstock.com/DavidTB

Illustration
Michael Fleischmann

Gestaltung & technische Umsetzung
Anna Bakalović und Annika Preyhs, Berlin

www.cornelsen.de

1. Auflage, 7. Druck 2021

Alle Drucke dieser Auflage sind inhaltlich unverändert und
können im Unterricht nebeneinander verwendet werden.

Druck: AZ Druck und Datentechnik GmbH, Kempten

ISBN 978-3-464-31852-2

PEFC zertifiziert
Dieses Produkt stammt aus nachhaltig
bewirtschafteten Wäldern und kontrollierten
Quellen.

www.pefc.de

PEFC/04-31-2260

Contents

 Madeleine (Laney)   Ken   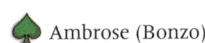 Ambrose (Bonzo)   Karen

Chapter 1 Laney introduces herself

It was, of course, a pity that Mum had to go into hospital a few days before the start of the school holidays. She had planned to come with us to Aunt Megan's, at least for the first two weeks of our summer holiday in Devon. But if she had come with us, I don't think she would have allowed us to do some of the things which we did. And if she had stopped us, we would never have had The Great Adventure, and you would not be reading this book now.

So let me introduce myself. My name is Madeleine. I don't like it much, but my parents didn't ask me before they chose it. My friends call me Laney. People who don't like me just call me Mad – which is what I am, sometimes. I'm fifteen years old and have short red hair, green eyes and a nice round face with a million freckles in summer, which is when this story starts. Oh yes, and I have a brother called Ken. I don't know whether you have a younger brother or sister, but if you do, I'm sure you'll agree with me that the most important letter in the word 'brother' is the 'r'. Without it, a brother becomes a bother.

Ken's OK really, but he's a boy (one minus point) and he's thirteen years old (two minus points). He's quite intelligent for a thirteen-year-old. He's as tall as me, with curly blond hair and he always has his nose in a book.

My mother is a teacher and my father ... is my father. He doesn't live with us any more, but we see him quite often. When Mum had to go into hospital, we went and stayed with him for a couple of days until Aunt Megan was ready for us. Then he drove us to Paddington Station and put us on the train for Devon.

"Behave yourselves while you're at your aunt's," he said. He always tells us to behave ourselves, though he doesn't always behave himself very well. But that's another story and nothing to do with our adventure.

5 "He never says 'enjoy yourselves'," said Ken, taking a fat book out of his rucksack.

"Never mind," I replied. "He doesn't enjoy himself much, so why should he hope that we do?"

"That's a very cynical thing to say. He enjoys his work."

10 Before we could start an argument, I took out my iPod and put the earplugs in my ears. We had a train journey of four hours ahead of us, and I didn't want to begin it with an argument.

Aunt Megan is Mum's sister. Her husband is a scientist
15 who works in a government laboratory in the west of England. They have two children the same age as Ken and me. They lived abroad for a long time and only came back to Britain last year, so I don't remember them at all. But Aunt Megan sounded very nice when I spoke to her on the phone
20 last week.

"Karen and Ambrose are looking forward to meeting you, Madeleine," she had said.

Ambrose! Yukk! What a name! Almost as bad as Madeleine!

25 "Please call me Laney, Aunt Megan," I had said. "All my friends do."

She had laughed. "Ambrose is a bit sensitive about his name, too."

"What shall I call him, then?"

30 "Call him Bonzo – all his friends do!"

I was looking forward to meeting my cousins and hoped that we would have a lot of fun together. They lived near a place called Tavistock on the edge of the Dartmoor National Park.

I looked across at Ken. He was still reading his thick book.

5 "What are you reading?" I asked. He was always reading something.

He looked up at me. " 'The Hound of the Baskervilles'."

"The what?"

" 'The Hound of the Baskervilles', Dumbo! It's a Sherlock
10 Holmes mystery story. It's all about Dartmoor – that's where we're going, isn't it? I want to get a bit of info about the place before we arrive."

" 'Hound of the Baskervilles'? Isn't that some kind of wild dog? I don't like dogs much," I said. "And anyway, Auntie
15 Megan and Uncle David don't live on Dartmoor."

"But it's not far away from Tavistock. And there are all kinds of strange and spooky things on the moor – like this huge ghostly dog, for example."

"Shut up, Ken! You know I don't like dogs."

20 "I'm getting hungry," said Ken, changing the subject. "Can't we get something to eat on this train?"

"Dad gave me £20 for food and drinks."

"OK. I'll have a hamburger or a bacon sandwich – no ketchup. And a Coke – please."

25 He dropped back behind his book.

"Aren't you coming with me?" I asked.

"I'll go next time," said the voice behind the book.

Older sisters can be a pain, especially when they are two years older.

Laney's OK – for a girl – but she sometimes thinks that she is so much better just because she's nearly two years older than me. Bossy is the right word for her! I suppose she expected me to go and get the food and drinks just because I said I was hungry. But I've just got to an interesting part of the book I'm reading. And I'm sure she's as hungry as I am. She's always hungry!

How can you go on holiday to a new place without finding out something about it before you go? Laney can do what she likes when we get there, but I'm going to go for long walks on Dartmoor. It sounds like a fantastic place. Open moorland and hills with no trees. Strange piles of rocks called 'tors' on the tops of some of the hills. Wild ponies which are sometimes swallowed alive by the dangerous bogs. Escaped convicts from the big prison at Princetown … well, maybe not nowadays. And at night the strange sound of the Hound of the Baskervilles. Oooer! I don't think I'd like to be out on the moor at night like Sherlock Holmes and Dr Watson …

"Here's your bacon sandwich. Put that book down and eat it while it's still hot."

Laney was back already.

"Eat what? The book or the sandwich?"

"The sandwich, Dumbo!"

She had already started eating hers.

"You've got ketchup all round your mouth. It looks like lipstick."

Laney's face went a bit red when I mentioned lipstick. She doesn't wear make-up – not much, anyway. But it's strange how sensitive girls can be even at the age of fifteen. She carefully wiped her mouth with a paper serviette and
5 sat down.

"Where are we?" she asked.

"Just past Swindon. Bristol is the next stop. It's still a long way to Devon. Haven't you brought a book to read or something?"

10 "No, but I've got a lot of text messages which I want to send."

She took out her mobile and started to tap out her messages. Last month her mobile bill was so high that Mum changed her tariff with the phone company. Now she can
15 send 500 free text messages a month – but she can only make calls to the Emergency Services and five selected mobile numbers: she can phone Mum, Dad, me and her two best friends Sharon and Carol. It's called a Teeny Text Tariff or something like that. Laney hates it. She can't phone
20 her friends, and if her friends don't ring her, she can't talk to them. And she's not very quick at sending texts. I think it would take her about a month to send all her 500 free messages! Most of her messages are the same, anyway: PLEASE GIVE ME A RING. But she sends: PLS GIV ME A O
25 and expects her friends to realize that the 'O' is supposed to mean 'ring'. But most of her friends are Dumbos. No wonder she doesn't get many calls!

My mobile account is still on track: I only made ten calls last month. Mum was very pleased, but I suppose ten calls a
30 month must make me the most boring thirteen-year-old in the world. But I don't care. I'm not like the others.

I picked up my bacon sandwich and turned back to my book.

"Yukk! It's covered in ketchup!" I cried. "I distinctly said 'no ketchup'!"

5   "Did you? I didn't hear you."

"No wonder. You've got your earplugs in! Daft bat!"

She threw her serviette at me, but missed by a mile.

Chapter 3   Bonzo introduces himself

It was Mum again, shouting up the stairs.

"We're going now, Ambrose. Are you sure you don't want to come with us to the station?"

"Quite sure," I shouted back. "I'm busy. I'm on the Net."

5 "It's rather rude, you know. You haven't seen your cousins since you were five. I'm sure they're looking forward to meeting you. Are you sure you won't change your mind and come with us?"

"We've had this conversation before, Mum!"

10 "But you're on holiday. School is over. You can't have any school work that is more important than meeting your London cousins. What are you doing up there, anyway? Are you on the Internet again?"

Yackety-yackety-yak! Don't mums ever stop talking?

15 I gave in and logged off.

"All right, Mum. I'll come with you on one condition."

"What's that?"

"You must tell Dad that I need a new computer."

"You can have one for your birthday."

20 "But that's in October!"

"Hurry up and get ready! We don't want to be late!"

Mum is a specialist in logic-free conversations. Dad is a chemist. I don't know what they have in common except Karen and me!

25 We drove off in the Range Rover. As a car, it's a bit of a gas-guzzler, but we need a four-wheel-drive where we live, and Dad gets his petrol cheap down at the laboratory where he works. So why not? Mum drove carefully down the hill to the main road and turned left for Plymouth. Karen was

sitting in the front (she says that she gets car-sick in the back), so I had the back seat to myself. It was summer, but the sun was behind the thick grey clouds that we seem to get all year round near Dartmoor. I don't know why the tourists
5   bother to come at all. We've been living here for over a year now, and it is quite a change from South Australia, where Dad's last job was. He doesn't talk much about his work. But it must be interesting and important, because it takes us around the world: I've been to five different schools in
10 Canada, the USA, New Zealand and Australia. We're real globetrotters. I don't see why Mum thinks our London cousins are so special. Compared with Adelaide, London's a boring place: no sea, no sunshine, no beach parties – a bit of a dump.

15   Still, I'm looking forward to meeting my cousins. I wish I knew more about them. I don't even know what they look like. Mum and Dad didn't have any photos of them, but it'll be nice to have a boy of my own age staying with us. We can sure have some fun if the weather gets a bit better.

20   I expect the girls won't mind if we boys spend most of our time together. Madeleine must be about the same age as Karen, so they'll want to do their own things, I expect.

I hope Madeleine likes the same sort of things that I like. I wish I had an older sister instead of an older brother. Bonzo's OK, but he's a boy and I can't expect him to have the same interests as me.

5   I wish Mum wouldn't drive so fast. We've been here over a year already, but I can't get used to driving on the left. Why can't the Brits drive on the right like everybody else? I don't think Mum is used to it, either. She nearly had a bad accident the first week we were here – driving on the wrong

10 side of the road – and it took her a while to get used to using the rear mirror: she kept looking out of the window at the sky instead of up at the rear mirror. It's on the other side of the car, of course.

"Must you drive so fast, Mum?"

15 "We're late, darling. And it's your brother's fault! He couldn't find his special trainers."

"It wasn't my fault!" shouted Bonzo from the back of the car. "I didn't want to come at all, remember? And who put my trainers in the washing machine anyway?"

20 "They were very dirty, darling. I wanted to wash them."

"You don't put £100 Adidas trainers in the washing machine, Mum!"

I wish they wouldn't argue so much. It makes me feel sick!

25 "Stop the car, Mum! I think I'm going to be sick."

"Jesus Christ!" came the voice from the back of the car. "What sort of wimp have I got for a sister."

"Be quiet, Ambrose!" said Mum, slowing down. "Open the window, darling. Get some fresh air. If I stop now, we'll never be at the station on time."

I opened the window and felt a little better. Sometimes I have to say things like that just to get a bit of attention. Nobody pays much attention to a thirteen-year-old girl when she's the youngest in the family. It's not fair.

A sheep wandered across the road right in front of us. Mum put the brakes on and missed the sheep by inches. She's a good driver, but I still think she drives too fast.

Bonzo said something nasty about the poor sheep and Mum told him not to use language like that again. She was not in a good mood. We were late and there was still ten miles to go. Mum switched the car radio on to listen to the traffic news.

"… accident on the A386 near the junction of the A38 just south of Crownhill. Long delays …"

"That's our route, isn't it Mum?" asked Bonzo from the back of the car.

"I'm afraid it is," said Mum. "But I think I know a short cut."

I groaned. Mum's short cuts are guaranteed to add half an hour to even the shortest trip.

"No, Mum …!" I squeaked.

"You heard: 'long delays'. We're late enough already," replied Mum, making a right turn in front of a large truck onto a very narrow road. "This will save us ten minutes on the normal route."

"I don't see why their dad couldn't have driven them down to Devon. It's only two hundred miles or so."

"This is not Australia, Ambrose," said Mum. "You don't drive fifty miles just to visit your neighbours in this country.

And anyway, their mum doesn't like them to have too much contact with their dad. They're divorced, you know."

"We know," said Bonzo. "And we'll try not to forget it."

Two more sheep walked slowly across the narrow road.
5 We just missed them.

"No lamb chops for lunch tomorrow," said Bonzo. That's just his sense of humour.

"Let's hope the London train is late. It usually is," was all Mum could think of saying.

10   The road was narrow and there were a lot of bends. Mum was driving fast. I began to feel car-sick again, but I said nothing. I just stuck my head out of the window and pretended to enjoy the drive.

It was four o'clock when we arrived at Plymouth station. The train was twenty minutes late.

Ken had nearly finished his big fat book and I had sent about fifty text messages without getting a *single* phone call. I was pretty fed up. And there was nobody waiting for us at the station. A lot of people got off the train, but most of them walked away or were met by friends and relatives. Within five minutes the train had left and the platform was empty except for a geeky-looking boy of about my age and a shy-looking girl of about Ken's.

No sign of Auntie Megan or our cousins.

"What now?" asked Ken.

"We wait."

We waited. More people came onto the platform and a local train came in. When it had left, the two kids were still standing on the platform. The geeky-looking boy with glasses was staring at me, so I turned away. I don't like boys looking at me too much.

"They didn't get on the train," said Ken, as if he was talking to himself. "You don't think …?"

"Of course not, Dumbo! Karen's fifteen and Bonzo's your age. And where's Auntie Megan? There's just the two of them."

"They look as if they're waiting for somebody. They keep staring at us."

"You're imagining things, Ken. Sit down and wait five more minutes. I've got a telephone number – a mobile number. It's Auntie Megan's, I think. If they're not here in five minutes we can buzz them and find out where they are."

The two strange kids came and sat down at a bench near ours. The boy got up and went to look at a train timetable on the station wall. The girl was staring shyly across at us. I ignored her. Where were our cousins and Auntie Megan? I was more fed up than ever now.

"Give me your mobile, Ken," I said at last.

"What?"

"I'm going to ring that mobile number and find out what's happened."

"Use your own phone."

"I can't – you know that. Or have you forgotten?"

"Sorry," he said, handing me his mobile. It's an old-fashioned thing. He must have had it for three years. He hardly ever uses it.

I rang the number and put the phone to my ear.

At the bench near us, the geeky-looking boy with glasses put his hand in his pocket and took out *his* mobile.

"Hello?" said the voice in my mobile and the boy on the bench at the same time. I put my hand over my left ear so that he wouldn't distract me.

"Who's that?" I asked suspiciously. It was not Auntie Megan. It was a teenage boy's voice.

"This," said the voice, "is Bonzo Rawlinson. Who the hell's that?"

It was an Australian voice. And he hadn't said 'hell'. He had used a much stronger word. I could feel my face going red. The geek on the other bench had started to shout, too, so I pushed my hand closer to my other ear and began again: "This is your cousin Laney here. We're on the platform at

Plymouth station waiting for you. We've been waiting here for fifteen minutes already. Where the hell are you?"

I used the right word. I don't use words like … like the *f*-word. At least not with people I don't know very well.

5 "Where are we? I'll give you three guesses!" he said in a voice that sounded almost like a laugh.

Ken was pulling at my arm now. What did he want? "Get off, Ken! I've got Bonzo Rawlinson on the phone." I put my hand over the phone and said to Ken: "He sounds like a real weirdo! He asked me to guess where they were! What a nerve!"

"Hello?" asked the voice. "Have you guessed where we are yet?"

"Are you trying to be funny? Stop it, Ken!" he was still pulling at my arm and laughing now. "What are you laughing at, Ken? Let go of my arm!" Then I turned my attention back to the weirdo on the mobile. "Let me talk to my Aunt Megan, please! I'm not into guessing games today!"

"Sorry. You can't talk to Mum," said the Australian voice. "She's looking for somewhere to park. The station car park was pretty full."

"You're at the station? That's great. Look, we're waiting for you down here on Platform 1, and we're pretty fed up … Shall we come out of the station and look for you, or what?"

"Don't bother, Sweetie," said the voice. "Just take your left hand away from your ear for a second and turn 45 degrees to your right."

I nearly dropped Ken's mobile in shock. How did he know that I had my hand to my left ear? I took my hand away and half turned round to find the face of the geek with glasses smiling at me from about six inches away. He closed his mobile and put it back in his pocket.

"You can end your call now," he said. "Save money and talk to your weirdo cousin direct!"

He must have heard every word I had said to Ken!

My face must have been as red as my hair. Dumbo Ken was doubled up with laughter on the bench beside me. The shy girl was slowly moving towards us. She looked almost as confused as me. A blond-haired woman was hurrying along the platform with her car keys in her hand.

"There must be some mistake ..." was all I could think
5   of saying.

Chapter 6 High Tor House ◆

"Just a small misunderstanding," Auntie Megan said to Laney as we drove northwards out of Plymouth. "That's what comes of losing touch with your sister for so long. Living abroad. Moving from place to place."

5 But this was not just a misunderstanding, I thought, squashed between Bonzo and Karen on the back seat of the Range Rover. It was a catastrophe for me. How can you forget the ages of your own sister's children? But then I remembered. It was Dad who had told us all about the
10 Rawlinson family after Mum had gone into hospital. All Mum had said was something like: 'Megan's got two children of your ages', which is a pretty vague statement. Dad must have mixed the two kids' ages up.

Stupid parent! I had been looking forward to some fun
15 with a boy of my own age, and what did I find? A boy nearly three years older than me with a shy little sister who would not be thirteen until her next birthday!

What a swiz! That's not the word I was using in my thoughts, and I know it's about 50 years out of date, but it
20 says everything! I felt really fed up – and I must have looked it, because the little girl next to me suddenly tried to get friendly: "Do you like ponies?" she asked.

WHAT a question! I liked computer games, and action films, and skateboards, and fast bikes. But as far as I knew, I
25 did NOT like ponies. I'd only ever seen them in books or on TV anyway.

Karen tried again: "I've got a lovely little pony called Snuggles."

I said nothing. Poor pony, with a name like that, I thought. But the girl went on: "You can ride him if you like …"

"Thank you very much." It sounded a bit cold without sounding cool. Perhaps I was being unfair on the poor girl. It was my turn to try starting up a conversation now. "Do you like reading?" I asked.

"Oooh, yes! I've read all the Harry Potter books."

Big deal. I'd read them when I was only eight. Karen was supposed to be nearly thirteen. What a wimp! Still, I wanted to be polite, so I tried again: "Actually, I'm reading 'The Hound of the Baskervilles' at the moment. It's a fantastic story!"

"Oh. Never heard of it. Is it about dogs? I love dogs! And ponies, of course."

That was the end of that conversation.

"Are you three all right in the back?" asked our Aunt.

"Fine, thanks, Auntie," I said. The others said nothing. Lucky Laney had the front seat. She had said nothing since we started, but perhaps she was thinking the same as me. This holiday was going to be one big flop.

We drove on for a long time in silence.

"Are we nearly there?" I asked. I knew that Tavistock was about twelve miles from Plymouth, but we had left the main road and were driving uphill now.

"Nearly there," said Aunt Megan. "Our address is Tavistock, but we don't live in the town. I'm sure you'll like it at High Tor House. It's closer to your uncle's work."

"He's a chemist, isn't he?" I asked. "What sort of work does he do?"

"Very important work," said the boy next to me – the boy who had a dog's name: Bonzo. "It's so important that he's not allowed to talk about it, even to us. He works in a

government laboratory out on the moors. He never talks about his work. The documents in his department are so sensitive that they're all marked TOP SECRET! DESTROY *BEFORE* READING!"

5   That was quite a funny thing to say. I even think I heard Laney laugh when he said it. Perhaps she didn't think he was such a geek after all. He was tall, and although he wore glasses, he had the sort of face which some girls might find attractive. He certainly had a sense of humour. Perhaps if
10 I tried hard, he might even like me enough to take me on those walks across the moors which I had been planning. I just hoped that Laney would want to do things with his kid sister so that we boys could spend most of our time together.

15   The car reached the top of the hill at last, and Aunt Megan stopped. In front of us were the rolling brown hills of Dartmoor – just like in my book – with the high rocks of the tors on many of them. To our right was a large house of grey stone.

20   "Wow!" said Laney. "What a lovely old house!"

It was almost the first thing she had said since we had left Plymouth.

I agreed with her. The house was not quite Baskerville Hall, but it would do.

Chapter 7   Slowly making friends

....

After I had got over the shock of the confusion of ages – Mum must have told us that Laney was my age, but I must have had a psychological block: perhaps I had just wanted Ken to be my age so that we could do things together.
5 The summer holidays aren't much fun if you haven't got many friends of your own age in the neighbourhood. And High Tor House has no neighbours. My nearest friends live in Tavistock, and that's five miles away.

But when Mum asked me to show our cousins around
10 the house while she was getting dinner ready, I began to think that Laney might be quite fun.

OK – she's a girl with short blonde hair and about a million freckles on her nose, but she has a sense of humour and laughs a lot. Her brother is a bit too serious for me. He
15 kept asking questions about the moor, and I couldn't answer all of them because we've only lived here for just over a year. I told him to ask Dad when he came home from work.

Karen asked Ken to go with her to feed Snuggles, but he didn't seem very keen. I'm not too keen on ponies myself,
20 but I felt a bit sorry for Karen. I thought Laney might want to go down to the stable with her, but she seemed keener to see the house – especially her bedroom.

*

If Bonzo had listened to me on the platform at the station, we wouldn't have had that embarrassing
25 scene with the phone call. I told him that we should look for a girl his age and a boy my age, but he just told me to shut up. Typical boy – or typical older brother, I should say,

because I don't mind boys, and Ken is quite nice. But I don't think he likes me much.

That must be because he was expecting Bonzo to be his age. I can't help that! It's not my fault that I'm only thirteen – and a girl!

When we got home, the first thing I had to do was to feed Snuggles. I asked Ken if he'd like to come with me, but he wanted to look around the house with Bonzo and Laney, so I went down to the stable on my own.

If I didn't have my pony as a friend, I would be very lonely. And I had been looking forward to making friends with a boy of my own age. I expect Laney is more interested in boys than ponies! Just my luck!

*

I can't believe my luck! My room has got the most wonderful view across the moors! It's smaller than Laney's, but her room hasn't got such a fine view. The hill across the valley is called King's Tor. The hill behind the house is High Tor, and the house is named after it.

The house must be a couple of hundred years old. I wonder if it has any secret passages. I must ask Uncle David when he comes home from work. He should know. Bonzo doesn't seem to know anything about the house. I don't think he likes it here on the edge of Dartmoor. He seems very Australian, though he was born in London, like me. I wish he were two or three years younger.

At least he has a sense of humour! The way he behaved at the station! As soon as Laney put her hand over her ear when he picked up the call, I knew it must be him. I tried to tell her, but she wouldn't listen. How embarrassed she was! I nearly died laughing! I wonder what Aunt Megan is going to cook for dinner? I hope it's something good. I'm so hungry I could eat a horse and chase the rider!

*

When I had got over the shock of that terribly embarrassing phone call on the station platform, I
5 found that I quite liked Bonzo. OK – he speaks English like an Australian, but he's the same age as me, and I don't see why we couldn't all have fun together. All four of us.

I know Ken can be a bit of a pain, but that's only because he's my brother, and we're together all the time. Maybe
10 the chemistry will be a bit different with four of us. Karen is the youngest, and seems a bit shy, and I don't expect that Ken will make her a good friend (he hates girls – even me sometimes!), but it will be my job to make sure that she doesn't get left out of everything.

15 If only she wouldn't talk about her pony all the time!

High Tor House is a fantastic place. My room is quite large and has a view of the garden, which is lovely. Ken has got the view of the moors. He can keep it!

Chapter 8   A walk to King's Tor ◆

"It's a wonderful morning," said Auntie Megan at breakfast. "Why don't you show your cousins the moor, Bonzo?"

I looked up from my cornflakes. Laney didn't seem very keen, but Karen seemed to think it was a good idea.

5   "Can we take sandwiches and things, Mum? We could have our lunch on the moor. Then we wouldn't be in your way. We can use Snuggles as a packhorse! He needs a long walk."

"What do you say?" asked Bonzo, looking across at Laney.
10   "The weather's good enough. We could walk to the top of King's Tor and have a picnic up there. Can we take Dad's binoculars?" He turned to me. "You can see all the way to the big prison at Princetown from King's Tor."

How did he know that I was so interested in Dartmoor
15   and the prison? Had Laney been talking to him about me?

I looked across at my sister. She was looking down into her cornflakes, but said: "That sounds like fun. Are you sure it's safe?"

"Safer than London," said Bonzo with a smile. "I hear
20   you've got a paedophile on every corner up there."

It was not a very tactful thing to say. Laney's face was starting to go red. It always does when people start talking about sex!

"Ambrose!" cried his mother in a shocked voice. She
25   seems to use his real name when she's angry with him. But the best reaction came from Karen.

"Oh do shut up, Bonzo, or we'll go without you! You're sex-mad!"

Now I thought I could see Bonzo's ears turning red. I looked at Karen with a little more respect.

The situation was saved by Laney, who burst out laughing.

5 "What I meant was will we be safe from wild animals and things?"

"As long as you stay close to the paths and don't wander off into a bog or something. Keep away from the very green grass."

10 "The Great Grimpen Mire!" I said dramatically.

"The *what*?"

"It's the big bog in my book," I went on. "There's a horrible scene in it where a moor pony falls into the Mire and is pulled down alive … until only his head is sticking out – and 15 it takes Sherlock Holmes and Dr Watson half an hour to pull the poor animal out again."

Halfway through my story I had seen Karen's face turn deadly white. She was thinking about Snuggles, of course. So I changed the ending. In the book, the pony is dragged 20 down to its terrible death in the Great Grimpen Mire! But that would be too much for a girl who has only just read the Harry Potter books, of course.

"Well, remember what I told you," said Auntie Megan. "Don't go far from the paths – and stay on the high 25 ground."

It was a good idea to take the pony, although he didn't seem too keen to carry all the things we took with us. Food and drinks and anoraks in case it rained suddenly and the binoculars and a couple of maps and my book, of course, 30 in case I got bored. And Laney's iPod and my camera … I almost felt sorry for the animal. Almost.

We set off down the valley towards King's Tor feeling a bit like explorers. It was a warm morning, and it got warmer as we walked down the narrow path into the valley.

"How far away is the top of King's Tor?" asked Laney. Was she getting tired already?

"Only about two miles," said Bonzo.

"Two miles!"

"Yeah. Do you think you can make it?"

Was he trying to be funny? Laney said nothing. She stuck out her chin and walked on, but I for one knew that she had never walked that far in her life before. Nor had I, but neither of us wanted our country cousins to know that we went everywhere by car in town.

After all, what's two miles?

Half an hour later, I had the answer: a hell of a long way.

First we followed a narrow path down the side of the hill and through a wood. At the bottom of the valley was a river about ten yards across. There was no bridge – just a few flat stones to walk on.

"That's the River Walkham," said Karen, leading Snuggles across. "We sometimes go fishing here."

Just as she was saying that, I saw a dead fish floating by. Karen stopped and watched it. I looked up the river and saw another dead fish on its way down.

"The water can't be very clean," I commented.

"There's nothing wrong with it," said Karen, defensively. "The fish taste good. You ate a couple of them for dinner last night."

"And they were delicious," I said. But the fish which floated past us didn't look very delicious. They looked very dead.

"We don't usually see dead fish in the river," Karen went on, thoughtfully. "The otters usually have them for lunch. Unless …"

"Unless what?"

5 "Oh, nothing … unless they're ill, I suppose. Walk on, Snuggles!"

We were walking uphill now, and soon we were out of the wood and on the moor. But the top of King's Tor still seemed a long way away. We were hot and thirsty, but I could tell 10 that Laney didn't want to stop until we had reached the top. She didn't want Bonzo to think we couldn't walk two miles. And nor did I.

We reached the top at last.

"Was that two English or two Australian miles?" Laney 15 asked.

Bonzo just smiled. "Sit down on that rock over there and have a drink," he said. "You've both done well – for townies!"

Of the five of us, Snuggles seemed to be the happiest. 20 Karen took the heavy bags off his back and just let him wander off to look for something to eat. I took the binoculars and walked around the rocks to get a better view across the moor. Bonzo came up behind me.

"That's Princetown on the horizon," he said. "Dartmoor 25 Prison is the big group of buildings on the left. The laboratory where Dad works is about a mile closer too us. Can you see it?"

I moved the binoculars downwards and saw a group of flat buildings with a high wire fence all around them. As I 30 was watching, a large road tanker came out of the main gate and drove away in the direction of Princetown.

"It all looks very secret," I said, handing the binoculars to Bonzo. "Doesn't your dad ever talk about his work?"

"No. If he did, he'd lose his job and probably go to prison. We don't talk about his work at home. It was the same in the States and in Australia."

"Do you miss Australia much?" I asked him.

"Yeah. Especially the sea. We're not far from the sea here in Devon. But it's not the same. You can't go swimming on Christmas Day. It's too cold for swimming even on Midsummer's Day."

"Lunch time!" shouted Laney. "Come on, you two!"

We sat down on the warm rocks in the sunshine and ate our sandwiches.

When I had finished, I took the binoculars and climbed up onto one of the big rocks at the top of the Tor. Looking to the west, I could see High Tor House on its hill two miles away. I followed the path we had taken down the hill and into the wood. I couldn't see the river, of course, because it was hidden by the trees, but just for a second or two I thought I could see something red moving between the trees. Not an animal, or a person. It looked like some kind of vehicle.

"What are you looking at, Ken?" asked Laney. "What's so interesting down there?"

"I don't know. It looks like a car or something."

"A car? But there's no road down there, Dumbo!"

"Let me look," said Bonzo, taking the binoculars. "And you're wrong, Laney. There is a road down there. It's only a narrow lane – not much more than a track, and it only goes from the main road to a couple of small farms down in the valley. We crossed it on our way up here. But only the farmers use it."

He handed the binoculars back to me. "I can't see anything. Probably just George Weldon in his old Land Rover."

"George Weldon?"

"He's our local Countryside Warden. He often comes up
5 here. He picks up the rubbish which the tourists leave and
things like that." He looked at his watch. "We'd better get
going. Go and get that pony of yours, Karen. I want to go
back home a different way – and show you a few things."

Chapter 9   A shock for Karen ♣

Snuggles was around the other side of the Tor. He usually comes to me when I call him, but today I had trouble catching him. He had wandered a long way off. I ran back to where I could see the others and shouted: "Bonzo! Don't wait for me! I'll go home the way we came! I've got a problem with Snuggles!"

Bonzo waved back to me and turned back to the others. They went on down the hill, and I went back for my pony.

Snuggles was very naughty. It took me twenty minutes to catch him, and I was very angry with him. But he just pushed his nose under my arm and snuggled – that's where he got his name from, after all – so I couldn't be angry with him for long.

I knew what Bonzo wanted to show the others. Dartmoor is covered with prehistoric buildings from the Stone and Iron Age. He's quite interested in history. I suppose he sees some connection between the Aborigines of Australia and the primitive people who lived here thousands of years ago. I'm not sure whether Laney and Ken are very interested in that sort of thing, but I knew I wouldn't be missing anything.

I walked Snuggles down the steepest part of the hill, but when we reached the wood, I got on his back. To be honest, I don't like long walks all that much. It was when I reached the lane that runs beside the river that I noticed something strange. Only the local farmers use this lane, and only when they have to. It only goes to a couple of farms and it stops at the last one. We had had some heavy rain a few days before, and there were fresh tyre marks on the track. Tyre marks that hadn't been there when we had crossed it a couple of hours before. Deep marks in the mud. The double wheels of a heavy truck.

Then I remembered that Ken had said he had seen something red moving along the bottom of the valley. But why would somebody want to bring a truck down a lane which didn't go anywhere?

Snuggles heard it before I did. He raised his head and moved a step backwards. Then I heard it, too. The noise of a heavy truck driving very slowly along the lane. I waited to see what would happen next. A minute or so later I saw it through the trees. It was a big red tanker, and it was backing slowly along the lane. A man was walking ahead of it, guiding the driver past the low branches. When he saw me, he waved to the driver to stop.

He walked over to me, smiling.

"Hello, little girl," he said. "What are you doing here?"

It seemed a strange question. I was just going to ask him what he was doing here. And I don't like people calling me 'little girl'. I know I'm only twelve and three quarters, but on top of Snuggles I was almost two feet taller than him.

I looked down at him and said: "I'm on my way home. I live up near High Tor."

The driver had got out of the truck and was walking towards us. He didn't look as friendly as the other man. Both of them were strangers to me, so my question: "Are you lost?" seemed natural enough.

"No," said the first man. "We've just delivered some fertilizer to the farm at the end of the lane. We couldn't turn the tanker, so we have to back out."

"Oh," I said. "You've been down to Mr Askew's farm?"

"That's right."

"Well, I'll get out of your way, then. Walk on, Snuggles!"

We crossed the river and I walked Snuggles off the path and into the trees. Then I stopped Snuggles and turned him round. I wanted to see what the men would do next.

The driver got back into the truck and started to back down the lane again. It was over a quarter of a mile to the

main road and there was nowhere to turn. And there was enough room to turn in the farmyard at the end of the lane. The milk tanker went there every evening and did not have to back out. I took the binoculars out of the saddlebag and
5 looked more closely at the big red tanker.

I had already seen the orange warning plate on the back of the truck, so I had some idea of what it was carrying. But it was the board on the side of the tank just behind the driver's cab that gave me the worst shock.
10   Chalked on it in great big letters was: XX 49.

Bonzo was talking almost all the time as we walked down the hill.

He was telling us all about the history of the people who had lived on Dartmoor thousands and thousands of years ago. Ken seemed quite interested, but I closed one ear and looked at the scenery as we walked. I had never realized that there were so many different shades of brown. Bonzo said something about the Australian Aborigines. They had twenty-five different words for 'brown' in their language because that was the main colour of the landscape. It was the same on Dartmoor too. There was not much green – only the trees. And on the hills there were not many trees.

We were walking along a wide track at the bottom of King's Tor now. Then the track began to turn to the right away from the Tor and towards the main road at the bottom of the valley. But the track didn't start to go downhill. It stayed level and started to lead around the side of a hill.

"Where does this track lead to?" I asked Bonzo.

"It goes all the way to Tavistock. But we're not going all the way."

"But the road to Tavistock is down in the valley."

"That's right. This is the track of the old railway to Princetown. It doesn't go up and down like a road. It stays as level as it can. It goes all the way round King's Tor and almost meets itself at the other side – over there," and he pointed across the valley between two hills. "It's now called the Dartmoor Way. Walkers use it a lot."

"What did you want to show us?" asked Ken.

"That," said Bonzo, pointing ahead.

We were halfway round the hill now and we could see it. The track was leading us towards a black hole in the side of the hill. A tunnel!

"Do we have to walk through it?" I asked.

5 "Unless you want to walk over the top," replied Bonzo. "You're not afraid of the dark, are you?"

"Of course not!" I said, although it wasn't quite true. I wasn't very keen on dark places, but I didn't want Bonzo to know that.

10 "It's not a long tunnel. You can see the other end quite clearly."

We walked on and into the tunnel. I was very dark inside. Ken seemed quite excited. He likes this sort of thing.

"Just imagine!" he said when we were almost halfway 15 through the tunnel, "just imagine a train coming down this tunnel towards us."

"Don't, Ken!" I said. Just the thought of it made me feel scared. I suppose that would be his idea of an adventure. But it isn't mine!

20 The walls of the tunnel were wet, and water was slowly dripping from the roof, but when we had got to the halfway point, the sound of flowing water which I had already noticed got louder.

"What's that sound?" I asked.

25 "When they were building this tunnel," Bonzo explained, "they hit an underground stream, so they had to build a drain to take the water out of the tunnel at the other end. Look!"

He pointed to a big pipe along the side of the track.

30 "The water comes out of the wall on the other side and goes under the old railway track and down this ... That's funny!"

"What?" asked Ken.

"Someone has taken the lid off he top of the pipe and forgotten to put it back properly."

In the light from the end of the tunnel we could see that
5 he was right. There was a large metal lid over an opening in the pipe, and it was only halfway across the opening.

"We must put it back or somebody will put his foot down the hole and break his leg," said Bonzo. "Come and give me a hand, Ken."

10 "I'll help you," I said quickly.

We both lifted one side of the lid – it was very heavy – and held it above the hole for a couple of seconds while we moved our fingers out of the way.

"I'll count to three," said Bonzo. "Then we must let go
15 at the same time. One … two … three!" As we dropped the metal lid back on the hole, we could both smell it. A strong chemical smell.

"Pooh! What's that smell?" asked Ken.

"Perhaps they've put disinfectant down the pipe. Perhaps
20 there are rats or something. Perhaps that's why the lid was off …" I said, but as I looked at Bonzo's face, I could see that he was frowning, and thinking hard.

"They wouldn't put disinfectant into an open stream," he said. "That's pollution. And it doesn't smell like disinfectant."
25 He thought for a minute. "I've smelt that smell before … Come on, you two, let's get out into the fresh air."

"Help!! Here comes the London Express!" shouted Ken, and started running towards the sunlight at the end of the tunnel. We followed him at the trot, happy to be leaving the
30 darkness.

I was glad to be out of the tunnel, but I hadn't been expecting the sight that was waiting for us there. The old

railway track came out onto a high bridge which crossed a small river. There were trees in the valley below. There were woods on the sides of the hills. The scenery was quite different from the brown moors at the other end of the
5 tunnel. Ken, who has no eye for scenery anyway, had run on ahead around the next bend in the track.

"Wow! What a surprise!" I cried. "Isn't it beautiful? What's the matter, Bonzo?"

He was looking down at the ground and frowning, but
10 said nothing. I looked down, too, and could see some deep marks between the small stones of the track. I looked up at Bonzo.

"A car?"

"No, these tracks were made by the tyres of a large van
15 or truck."

Ken was now walking slowly back to us.

"Come on, you slowcoaches!" he cried. But then he saw that we were looking down at the ground. "What are you two staring at?"

20 "Tyre tracks," said Bonzo quietly.

"From the Land Rover I've just seen, I expect," said Ken. "It's parked at the side of the track just around the bend."

We walked over the bridge and saw that he was right. Just behind a couple of trees there was a green Land Rover.
25 On its side were the words 'Countryside Warden'.

"It's George Weldon's," said Bonzo. "But where is he?"

"I'm here," said a voice behind us. We turned round to see a tall, dark-haired man with blue eyes and a nice smile. He was wearing shorts and big rubber boots, and his legs,
30 arms and face were dark brown from working out of doors in the summer sunshine. He looked very fit. So this was the Countryside Warden.

"Who are your friends?" he asked in a friendly way.

"My cousins: Laney and Ken."

"Pleased to meet you," said George, shaking hands with us. "Are you enjoying your holiday here?"

5 "I told George you were coming," said Bonzo. "Don't look so surprised, George. I got it wrong. Laney is my age and Ken is Karen's."

"Where is your little sister, anyway?" he asked, looking around.

10 "She's gone home the way we came. She's got her pony with her, so maybe it's better she didn't come with us through the tunnel. George," he asked. "Have you been inside the tunnel today?"

"No. Why?"

15 "Well, come and look at this."

We walked back over the bridge and showed him the tyre tracks.

"These tracks were made by a heavy truck," he said. "Look – it had double wheels at the back. And I'm the only person 20 who's allowed to drive down the Dartmoor Way. It's part of my job. All other vehicles are strictly prohibited. Anyway, the old bridge isn't safe for anything as heavy as this."

I was expecting Bonzo to tell him about the lid on the pipe inside the tunnel, but he said nothing. So I mentioned 25 it. Bonzo gave me an angry look which I couldn't explain. Why should he be angry with me?

George began to look even more serious. At last he said: "Come with me, but be careful: the path is steep and slippery." He led us down the side of the hill and under the 30 bridge to the river at the bottom. "Look at that!" he said.

We looked.

In a small pool under the bridge, where the water was not flowing very fast, we saw ten or twelve dead fish.

We looked at each other.

"I found them like this a few minutes ago," George went on. "A fisherman down at Horrabridge told me that he'd seen quite a few dead fish in the river, so I've been taking samples of the water for testing."

"What could have killed the fish?" asked Ken.

"It must be some kind of pollution," said the Countryside Warden. "Somebody is poisoning the water in the river. And this isn't the first time."

"Who would want to do that?" I asked, shocked.

We all looked at each other, but nobody said anything. I looked especially closely at Bonzo. He was looking down at his shoes, saying nothing. Why had he looked so angry when I had told George about the lid on the pipe in the tunnel? Was Bonzo hiding something?

"When will you have the results of the tests?" asked Ken.

"The samples will have to go to the laboratory at Princetown," said George. We should have the results in a week."

Suddenly Bonzo looked up. "The lab where Dad works? Is that where you're sending them?"

"Of course. It's the nearest place. Why?"

"Oh … nothing."

But there was something – I knew he was holding something back. What could it be? Was it something to do with his dad's laboratory? But George noticed nothing. He was telling us how he had spent the morning.

"I took the first sample below the bridge at Horrabridge, and I've taken six or seven more."

"Why so many?" I asked.

"The concentration of the poison or pollutant will be stronger as we get nearer the source," said George. "And if there is no pollutant in one of the samples, we'll know that the place where the pollutant is being put into the river is below the place where we took the sample. Then we can concentrate on that part of the river."

"Clever!" said Ken. "Can we help you, please?"

"I'm afraid not," George was very serious now. "This is official business – my job. But you can do one thing for me."

"What's that?" asked Bonzo, suddenly taking an interest.

"The River Walkham runs down the valley below your house. I expect you'll be out of doors quite a lot in the next few weeks. Keep a pencil and a piece of paper in your pocket at all times. If somebody is polluting the river, they'll choose a quiet place – and they may do it at night. If you notice anything unusual – a truck down by the river or something like that – try to get its number. Do you all have mobiles?" We all patted our jeans pockets. "Good. I'll give you my mobile number and you can ring me at any time."

"Day or night?" asked Ken, quite excited now.

"Well, I don't expect you to be on watch all night, but you can certainly ring me at any time, day or night, if you see something really suspicious. But if you see anything suspicious, you mustn't do anything yourselves. Phone me first – and be careful!"

And he walked off, following the tracks of the vehicle into the tunnel.

Chapter 11   Ken and Karen put
two and two together

When we got back to High Tor House it was teatime, and Karen was waiting for us in the kitchen. Auntie Megan had gone to visit a friend in Tavistock, and Uncle David was not back from work yet. So there were no adults in the house to
5   listen to our plans – and perhaps stop us.

Before we went into the kitchen, Laney pulled me back and whispered: "Be careful what you say to Karen and Bonzo. Something strange is going on here, and I think Bonzo knows more about it than he's told us. I don't really
10   trust him. And Karen is his sister."

"What do you mean?" I asked, surprised.

"Well, when I started telling the Countryside Warden about the pipe in the tunnel, I felt that Bonzo didn't want me to talk about it. He gave me such an angry look. There
15   was a chemical smell in the tunnel, and Uncle David is a chemist …"

"And you think there's a connection?"

"I'm not sure. But I think we should be careful. And it'll be interesting to see Karen's reaction to our news. She's
20   missed all the fun so far!"

But if we thought we were the only ones with news, we were wrong.

When we went into the kitchen, Karen was already talking to Bonzo. She stopped when she saw us.

25   "I was just telling Karen about what's happened," said Bonzo. "And she's got some news for us, too. Tell them, Karen."

"When Snuggles and I reached the river, we saw a big tanker backing down the lane …"

"*Backing* down the lane?" asked Bonzo, astonished. "Why on earth …?"

"Don't interrupt me, Bonzo," Karen went on. "If you've got any questions, ask them later. This truck was backing down the lane. One man was driving and another was walking ahead of him. When he saw me, he asked me what I was doing there. I could have asked him the same! Anyway, he told me some story about delivering fertilizer to the farm at the end of the lane."

"Well, perhaps he was."

"Oh, *do* shut up, Bonzo, and let me tell it!"

Karen could get quite angry when she wanted to. I was beginning to feel more respect for my cousin now.

"Sorry, Karen. Please go on."

"Thank you. Well, I simply couldn't believe them, could I? There's plenty of room to turn at the farm, isn't there? They wouldn't need to back the tanker all the way to the main road. Maybe they thought I was just another stupid girl. But they fell into my trap. 'Oh,' I said: 'You've been down to Mr Askew's farm?'."

Here Karen made a dramatic pause and looked at us in triumph.

"*What did they say then?*" asked her brother.

"What did they say then?" Karen repeated her brother's words as if he had said something very stupid indeed. This was not the reaction she had been expecting. She was disappointed. "It's not what they *said*, Bonzo. Everything they *said* was a lie! How long have we been living here? A year? Nearly two years? And you *still* don't know the names of our closest neighbours! The name of the farmer who lives at the end of that lane is not Askew but *Andrews!*"

Even Bonzo looked at her with respect.

"Well done, Karen! They really fell into your trap!"

5 "So," said Laney. "We know that somebody has been polluting the river – George Weldon has already told us that – and you saw this tanker backing down the road beside the river. It must have gone halfway down the lane and dumped something in the river. It couldn't go down to the farm to

10 turn because it had no business being there at all. I wonder what was in it?"

Now it was my turn.

"Was it a red tanker?" I asked.

"Yes, it was." Then she looked suspiciously at me. "How

15 did you know that?"

"When we were up on top of King's Tor, I saw a red tanker going down the road towards Princetown. Perhaps it was the same one." I looked straight at Bonzo before going on: "It came from your dad's laboratory, Bonzo."

20 Nobody spoke for quite a while. But we were all thinking the same thoughts. Finally Bonzo said: "But it may have been a different tanker. There are plenty of red tankers on the roads."

"Wait a minute!" cried Laney. "When we were up on top of

25 King's Tor, Ken said he saw something red moving between the trees. Remember? That must have been about a quarter of an hour after he saw the truck leave the laboratory. So it was probably the same truck."

Bonzo was still not convinced.

30 It was Karen who finally convinced him.

"They're right, Bonzo. I haven't told you everything yet. There was an orange plate on the back of the tanker – you know what that means: dangerous chemicals."

"So somebody's dumping dangerous chemicals into the river. A red tanker. It could be from anywhere, couldn't it?"

"Not with XX 49 chalked on the side," said Karen. "That's the number of the lab where dad works."

Chapter 12   Uncle David ♠

They were right. I had known it the moment I smelt the chemicals that somebody had put down the pipe in the railway tunnel. But I still couldn't believe that Dad had anything to do with it.

5   I couldn't believe that he would do anything to pollute the environment. I didn't know much about his work – he wasn't allowed to talk about it anyway – but I was sure that Dad would never do anything wrong. When I looked at Laney and Ken, however, I could see that they were not so
10 sure.

    They had only seen Dad at dinner yesterday evening. He had been pleased to see them, but he hadn't said much during the meal. Perhaps he had been thinking about problems at work. Were they having problems down at the lab? Waste-
15 disposal problems? Was there any way we could find out from him without actually asking him about his work?

    Laney was looking hard at me now. I had to say something.

    "I know what you're thinking," I said, "but you're wrong.
20 I'm sure Dad knows nothing about any pollution. But maybe we can find out something about what they do with their waste at the lab without actually asking him about his work there."

    "I think I have an idea," said Laney. "Leave it to me."
25 So I did.

*

Dad came home as usual at about 6.30.

"Hello, everyone," he called out when he came into the hall. "What's for dinner?"

"Something special," called Mum from the kitchen. "Your favourite spaghetti Bolognese! Ready in ten minutes!"

5 Dad came into the kitchen and kissed Mum quickly on the cheek, like he always does when he comes home.

"Mmmm! It smells marvellous!" he said. "I'll just get changed. I'll be down in five minutes."

He looked tired but not worried. He had probably had a
10 hard day. He always got changed as soon as he arrived home because the clothes he wore at work always smelt slightly of the chemicals they used in the lab. He loved his work but tried to keep it separate from home life.

Ten minutes later the six of us were all sitting round the
15 big kitchen table. Mum makes the best spaghetti Bolognese this side of the Alps, and today's dinner was no exception. For the first ten minutes, everybody was too busy eating to speak, but while Mum was in the kitchen with the plates of those who wanted a second helping, Dad asked us about
20 our day.

The four of us had agreed to say nothing about pollution, but he brought the subject up himself.

"George Weldon came up to the lab with some samples of water from the River Walkham," he began. "He wanted
25 us to test them. He said he'd seen you walking along the Dartmoor Way."

"There were dead fish in the river," said Karen without looking up from her empty plate.

I nearly kicked her under the table, but I suppose George
30 would have told Dad what he suspected.

"I expect there were," said Dad, half angrily. "Every time they find pollution in the rivers or lakes near here, they think it comes from our lab. But it doesn't. We're very careful – we have to be."

Mum came back with our second helpings, but Laney hadn't wanted any more to eat. She wiped her lips with her serviette, sat back in her chair and smiled sweetly at Dad. 'Leave it to me,' she had said.

I wondered what she was going to say.

"We're doing a project on pollution at school," she began, "and one of our summer tasks is to find out anything we can about pollution and waste disposal. Well, Uncle David, we seem to be in the middle of a pollution mystery on our first day here. It's quite exciting. I can write about the Countryside Warden's job and about what Mr Weldon was doing today – I'm sure it's nothing to do with your laboratory or he wouldn't take the samples to you for checking, would he?"

Clever girl, I thought. She smiled her nicest smile at Dad. I waited for what she would say next. Would she ask Dad to invite us up to the lab? Impossible! Not even Mum had ever been inside.

Dad didn't answer her question, but he stopped eating and looked sharply at her for a second.

"Go on, Laney. How can I help you with your project?"

"Well, I know you can't tell me anything about what you do in your secret laboratory," she smiled again. "But perhaps you could tell me something about the lab's waste disposal arrangements."

She sat back in her chair and waited.

"Well, that's no secret," said Dad, smiling back at her. He was in a good mood after his good meal. "We recycle many of our waste products – especially any dangerous ones – at the lab itself. Of course, there's quite a lot of waste which we can't or don't handle at the lab because it isn't much more dangerous than any ordinary industrial waste from a factory."

"So what happens to it?" asked Laney.

"A big tanker truck comes round once a week and takes
it to a recycling company in Tavistock. They came today, actually."

"And what do *they* do with it?"

"They recycle it – I suppose ..." Dad spoke the last two words rather slowly and stopped in the middle of his sentence. He looked hard at Laney and went on: "We fill the waste into their tanker, the driver signs for it and drives away. As soon as the recyclers have signed for it, it's their responsibility. That's about all I can tell you."

"Thank you, Uncle David," said Laney sweetly. "That was all very interesting and helpful."

If Dad suspected anything, he said nothing. And when Karen brought in the dessert – strawberries and thick Devon cream – his thoughts turned back to food.

Well done, Laney, I thought as I started to eat my strawberries. Now I know what to do next.

Chapter 13　A trip to Tavistock ♣

It was clever of Laney to get all that information out of Dad without telling him what we knew about the big red tanker truck! Who says girls aren't as clever as boys? *Answer: Boys.* Never mind. I'm not prejudiced. That was just a joke.

5　The following day Bonzo looked up chemical recycling companies in Tavistock in the Yellow Pages. There was only one, and the advert took up almost half a page: ENVIRONMENTAL PROCESSORS (TAVISTOCK) Ltd, Waste Minimization & Recycling Services, Liquid Wastes, Special

10　Wastes. Saving the Environment. Government Departments Served.

One of the 'government departments' would be Dad's laboratory, of course. There was a phone number and an address – an industrial estate on the other side of town. At

15　the bottom of the advert was the green 'recycling' symbol and a picture of a big red tanker truck.

"That's them!" I cried, pointing to the picture of the tanker. "I'm sure that's the tanker I saw down by the river."

"What a pity you didn't take its number when you saw

20　it," said Ken.

"I didn't know it was so important at the time, did I? I knew nothing about the pollution in the river until you three came home at teatime!"

"Don't worry, Karen," said Bonzo. "You did everything

25　else right. If those men were dumping stuff in the river, you did the right thing not to ask them what they were doing. Men like that can be dangerous if they're caught – or if they think they're going to be caught. But we can be sure of one thing now."

"What's that?" asked Laney.

"Dad told us that they only collect waste from the lab once a week, OK? And the water in the river was polluted *before* Karen saw the red tanker. We know that because the fisherman at Horrabridge reported dead fish in the river before Ken probably saw the truck driving down the lane this morning when we were up on King's Tor. And somebody had put chemicals into the pipe in the tunnel we walked through – probably several days before: that might be what killed the fish." He looked at each of us in turn over the top of his glasses, which were almost on the end of his nose. This always happens when Bonzo gets excited about something. "So what does that tell us?"

Nobody spoke.

"Come on, come on! Use your intelligence."

"It means that the red tanker is not just dumping stuff from Dad's lab!" I called out.

"Exactly."

"So what do we do now?" asked Ken. "Tell the police?"

Bonzo thought for a minute before replying. "I think the police would need more evidence than a story from the four of us. But we can phone George Weldon and tell him. He drives around the countryside all the time. That's his job. He can keep an eye open for the red tanker."

So that's what we did.

The next day was a Wednesday – market day in Tavistock. Mum does her shopping in town on a Wednesday, and she was quite surprised when we told her that we all wanted to go to Tavistock with her.

"There won't be much room for my shopping if you all come!" she said. "And I'm having lunch with my friend Ella today."

"Don't worry, Mum," said Bonzo. "I want to show Laney and Ken the town. We can grab a hamburger or something at MacD's and meet you back at the car after lunch."

"All right," said Mum, and we piled into the car.

5 What we didn't tell her was that Bonzo and Laney had worked out a plan. We wanted to have a closer look at ENVIRONMENTAL PROCESSORS (TAVISTOCK) Ltd.

Tavistock is a typical West Country town on the River Tavy. There are lots of lovely old buildings, so Mum couldn't
10 really be surprised that we wanted to show it to our cousins. It's also a shopper's paradise at any time, and on market day it's always very full. It took Mum a quarter of an hour to find a parking space in one of the car parks. And we were in luck, because the car park was on the far side of town, near
15 the industrial estate. Mum took the Park-and-Ride bus into town, but we said we would walk.

As soon as the bus had left, we turned our backs on the town and walked off towards the industrial estate.

ENVIRONMENTAL PROCESSORS was the biggest
20 company on the estate. There were two or three large buildings and *dozens* of red vehicles with a high fence around the whole site. About ten of the vehicles were big red tankers.

"Well!" said Laney when she saw them. "What do we do
25 now?"

Bonzo thought for a minute. Then he thought for another minute. Then he gave up. "Any ideas?" he asked. Very democratic, I thought.

Ken had the best idea. "We can't start following red
30 tankers around Devon," he began. "We can only wait for another tanker from the lab and watch where it goes. That

will give us a day, a time and a place to start looking. Where's your map, Bonzo?"

Bonzo took his map of the area out of his rucksack and handed it to Ken. Ken opened it in the middle and looked at the towns and the roads.

"Here's Tavistock – and here's Princetown. Where's your dad's lab on the map, Karen?"

I showed him.

"OK. The tanker comes from Tavistock and is loaded at the lab. It's supposed to drive back to Tavistock from there. It can either go this way, through Horrabridge, or this way, through Princetown and Merrivale. You know the roads, Bonzo. Which way would *you* go?"

"Princetown is shorter."

"Right. Now we know where they dumped the stuff because Karen saw them – here," he put his finger on the narrow lane. "And we know that some waste from somewhere else must have gone into the river a day or two before we saw the truck. That might have gone into the river near Merrivale. I don't think they had been down the narrow lane before. They certainly won't try that again. Karen's seen them and they probably didn't know that there was nowhere to turn."

"But surely somebody would have seen them dumping the stuff near Merrivale," said Laney.

"Not if they did it *at night!*" said Bonzo suddenly. "Look at all those tankers over there. How do we know whether they're full or empty? Maybe they get rid of some of the stuff in the middle of the night. That would be much easier. Especially if they wanted to drive along the Dartmoor Way and put stuff down the pipe in the tunnel! Nobody would see them at night!"

It was then that I saw him.

The man who had been walking in front of the red tanker down the lane the day before. He had come out of one of the buildings and was walking over to one of the tankers.

"That's him!" I squeaked in excitement. "That's the man I saw – the man who saw me!"

"Quick!" said Bonzo. "Hide! He mustn't see you, Karen."

5   I quickly ran behind one of the trees near the fence.

Just as he was getting into the tanker, the driver saw the others and walked over to the fence.

"Clear off, you kids!" he said in a very unfriendly way. "This is private land. Some of these tankers are full of very
10 dangerous chemicals. You wouldn't want to get hurt, would you?"

It sounded very much like a threat. I was glad he hadn't seen me!

The others said nothing. They turned away and began
15 to walk back towards the main road. The driver got into the tanker and started up. I saw Laney put her hand in her pocket and pull out a piece of paper. She was going to write down the number of the truck.

The gate opened, and the tanker slowly drove out of the
20 yard and past the others. When the tanker had turned right into the main road, I caught them up.

"Did you get the number?" I asked.

"Of course: Y814TDW."

"Thirteen," said Bonzo quietly. "If you add up the numbers
25 you get 13. Not a very lucky number."

"What now?" asked Ken.

"A walk around town and then lunch," said my big brother. "That's all we can do today. Then we must work out a plan."

Chapter 14   Working out the plan

The weather was good for the next few days, so we had no problem in putting our plan into action.

I have never cycled and walked so far in all my life. Karen, Ken, Bonzo and I must have cycled or walked up and down
5 every lane within three miles of High Tor House in the five days from Thursday to the following Monday.

Our plan was a very simple one.

If the tanker driver wanted to dump the industrial waste from the laboratory somewhere between the lab
10 and Tavistock, he would need to find a place that was fairly hidden but near a stream or river. A place where he would not be disturbed. There were a lot of places like that.

On Thursday, Bonzo and I took the bikes – Karen's was a bit small for me – and cycled from Merrivale to Princetown,
15 which is about four miles. Ken and Karen walked down to Sampford Spiney to check the narrow road to Horrabridge. They would have the bikes the following day while Bonzo and I did some walking.

The big prison is right in the centre of Princetown and it
20 looks very depressing. It's a star-shaped group of old grey buildings with a high wall around it. I wouldn't like to be a prisoner there. If we caught anybody polluting the river, would he be sent here? The thought worried me a little, and I talked to Bonzo about it.

25 "People who break the law have to be punished," was all he said.

He was right, of course, and I felt better when he said that.

There were only two lanes leading off the road between Merrivale and Princetown which a tanker could use. We had decided to count them on our way out and cycle up them on our way back. I told Bonzo that I was hungry, so we
5 had a snack in Princetown before cycling back.

We turned left down the first lane. After about a mile, we came to a big quarry. Bonzo looked at the map.

"Foggintor Quarry," he said. "This would be a good place to dump industrial waste. Let's have a look around."
10 We did, but we found nothing. Bonzo said that this made the quarry a likely place for a visit from the red tanker.

"They wouldn't go to the same place twice," he said, and I agreed.

The only other lane went steeply up the hillside of Little
15 Mis Tor to the north of the road. It was about a mile to the top, but we decided not to cycle up there. There were no trees on the hillside, and the lane could be clearly seen from the road. It could only be used for dumping at night.

"Home now?" I asked, feeling a bit tired.
20 "Let's just try the other side of Merrivale," suggested Bonzo. "Unless you're too tired, of course."

"Me? Tired? Of course not!"

So we cycled through Merrivale and down the road towards Tavistock for about two miles and only found one
25 track – a very narrow one – across Whitchurch Common towards Feather Tor. We cycled down it to Moortown, which is not a town but a very small village, and cycled home from there.

When we got back to High Tor House, Ken and Karen
30 were sitting outside in the garden and having tea with Auntie Megan. She had baked some scones and a cake. When she

went into the kitchen to get us something to drink, Karen quickly told us what she and Ken had done.

"We walked down to Sampford Spiney and on towards Horrabridge, but there are quite a lot of houses down there, and people would notice a tanker truck going up the road from Horrabridge. So we crossed the river at Ward Bridge and went up the hill past Eggworthy Farm. But that hill is probably too steep for a heavy tanker. There's a lane on the left that leads to Daveytown, which isn't a town – just a couple of houses, and another on the right to Routrundle near the old railway."

"That's a likely place," said Bonzo thoughtfully. "The track goes on to the Princetown-Horrabridge road. But the farmer at Routrundle, old Mr Dawson, wouldn't let a tanker truck drive across his land. George Weldon told me all about him. He lives alone and chases any strangers away from his farm. He's a bit of a nutter, they say."

"Look out," whispered Ken. "Here comes your mum."

So we had to wait until later to finish our discussions.

*

On Friday, Ken and Karen took the bikes while Bonzo and I went for a walk around High Tor just in case we had overlooked any possible dumping places.

When Ken and Karen came back, we went up to Bonzo's bedroom and marked all the likely dumping places on the map. There were seven – possibly eight of them.

How could the four of us be in seven or eight places at the right time?

"We'll have to split up," Bonzo decided. "We've all got mobiles, and we've all got George Weldon's mobile number. Should we tell him about our plan?"

"I think it would be more fun to keep it to ourselves," said Ken.

"It would be more fun," Bonzo agreed, "but I don't think we can do everything on our own. We've got a plan. We've got binoculars and mobiles, bikes and a pony, but we need someone with a car as well."

"Bonzo's right," I said. "If we want to catch them red-handed, we'll need proof – and the police."

So Bonzo rang George Weldon and told *him* about our plan. Then he listened for a long time while George told him something. Finally he finished his phone call. When he had finished, he was smiling.

"What did George say?" I asked. I hate secrets – unless they're mine, of course – and I knew that George must have told Bonzo something quite important.

"George has got a surprise for us," he said. "He wants to meet us at the main road in half an hour."

"But what did he *say!*"

"I told you, Laney. It's a surprise. Don't you like surprises? Put your walking shoes on and come along with us. Don't be so impatient!"

There were times when I felt like knocking Bonzo's glasses off the end of his silly nose, and this was one of them. But I didn't, of course. He was right. I *was* impatient, and this might be a bad thing, because in our adventure we would need to be patient. So I put on my walking boots and went down to the main road with the others.

George Weldon was waiting for us there. He was standing right beside the main road.

"Come over here," he called, "and look back up the lane. Tell me if you notice something new."

We walked over to the main road, turned around and looked.

We saw the lane, and the trees, and the sign which said 'High Tor House only', and the 'no through road' sign on its
5 post, but I couldn't see anything new.

It was Ken who noticed it first.

"There's a new sign on the post. What does it mean?"

"It means what it says," said George with a smile. "This road is closed to any vehicle heavier than 7.5 tonnes. The County
10 Highways Department has been promising for a long time to put up these signs on most of the lanes in the area and at last they've done it. When I told them about the dead fish, they decided to start putting up the signs right away. They should help to stop pollution. If a heavy tanker like the red one you
15 saw drives up one of these narrow roads, it's breaking the law now. The driver doesn't even have to dump any waste – he could easily lose his driving licence just by driving past this sign!"

"Cool!" said Ken.

20 "Well, it's a clear warning," said George, looking serious now. "No more heavy trucks on these narrow lanes. Now tell me some more about your plan."

"We're planning to keep an eye on any lanes between here and Princetown where we think the tanker might go,"
25 said Bonzo. "One of us will be on top of King's Tor. He or she will see the tanker leaving the lab on Tuesday and will phone the others. They will be down on the road to Tavistock, about a mile apart. Then we wait and see how far the tanker goes before it turns off the main road."

30 "And if it doesn't turn off? If it goes straight to Tavistock?" asked George with a smile. "What then?"

"We try again next week," I said. "We will have to be patient."

Bonzo smiled at me. I could have kicked him!

"And then you phone me," said George, "and I'll phone
5 the police. But remember: people who break the law can be very dangerous. Don't try to stop the truck yourselves!"

"Of course not!" we all said at once.

George Weldon looked at us as if he couldn't quite believe us.

Chapter 15   General Ken

When the others told me about my part in the plan, I was not pleased.

"It's not fair!" I cried. "I'll miss all the fun!"

"No you won't, Ken," said Bonzo. "You'll have the
5 most important job. You'll be on top of King's Tor with the binoculars. Your job will be to tell us which way the tanker goes. You'll be our General – General Ken. You'll see almost everything from up there, and you can take my mountain bike with you. Then you'll be able to cycle down and join us.
10 And you won't be far from Karen."

"And where are you going to put *me?*" asked his sister.

"Your post will be near the lane that leads to Routrundle," said Bonzo, who was beginning to sound a bit like Field Marshal Bonzo, in charge of the whole campaign.

15 "And where will you and Laney be?"

"We'll be on the main road – there are only two likely places there."

"Big deal!" cried Karen. "You've put yourself and Laney in the best places! I suppose you want me just to be little
20 Corporal Karen again!"

"I've given you the most important post," said Bonzo, sounding a little hurt. "And you can take Snuggles with you. You'll be the only one on the Horrabridge side. So if the tanker goes that way, you'll have the job of contacting George
25 Weldon. We two will be miles away. Ken will probably be able to cycle down and join you. If the tanker goes that way, it's us who'll miss all the fun!"

I felt that I could *almost* believe him, and even Karen seemed to be happy when he mentioned Snuggles.

So now we knew what we had to do, and it all seemed so easy. If we had known what would happen, we would probably have waited a week.

On Saturday and Sunday Uncle David was at home, and we went for a couple of trips in the car. We had wonderful weather all weekend, but on Sunday evening dark clouds came up from the south-west, and it turned quite cold.

On Monday it rained all day.

We sat around the house hoping for good weather, but none came.

"Do you think we should wait until next week?" asked Laney.

"No," said Bonzo. "The weather forecast for tomorrow is good. If it stops raining during the night, we can go ahead."

When I woke up the following morning, I ran to my bedroom window and looked out. It had stopped raining, but there were still low, heavy clouds over the tops of the Tors. I could see King's Tor clearly, but the clouds were very low.

I remembered something I had read in 'The Hound of the Baskervilles' and hoped that it wouldn't happen.

At eleven o'clock, Laney and Bonzo took their bikes and cycled down the hill towards Merrivale, Karen rode off on Snuggles, still looking a bit unhappy and I, General Ken, set off for King's Tor with the binoculars. I wasn't feeling happy, either, but for a very different reason: the weather.

I reached the top of King's Tor and sat down on a large rock from which I could see the moor almost as far as Princetown.

At twelve fifteen I saw the red tanker arriving from Princetown. It drove behind one of the buildings, and I picked up my mobile. I dialled Bonzo's number.

"The tanker's arrived," I said. "It must be filling up now."

"Good," said Bonzo. "We're ready down here. I'll ring Laney if you ring Karen."

5 "OK."

I rang Karen's number and she answered right away. She must have been holding her mobile in her hand!

"General Ken here," I said. "The red tanker's arrived and is filling up now. Are you ready down there?"

10 "Yes, General!" said Karen. She sounded happier now. "We're ready."

"We?"

"Snuggles and me, Dumbo!"

"OK. Stand by for action in about one hour's time."

15 "Aye-aye, sir!" and she rang off.

That sounded like the wrong thing to say to a General, I thought. 'Aye-aye' was what you said to a captain in the navy, wasn't it?

The clouds were getting lower and there was still no
20 movement down at the lab. I looked at my watch again. Twelve thirty-five. Perhaps it would take them half an hour to fill the tanker.

Then the worst thing in the world happened.

The tops of the hills on the other side of Princetown began
25 to disappear! The clouds were rolling down the hillsides as a thick, white mist. I had read about these moorland mists in 'The Hound of the Baskervilles' and knew what to expect.

I picked up my mobile and dialled Laney's number.

"Hi, General!" She could see my name on her display, of
30 course.

"The mist is coming down," I said, trying to sound drama-tic rather than worried. "The high hills behind Princetown have disappeared already, and the clouds are getting lower all the time."

"It's OK here," she told me. "Any sign of the tanker?"

"No."

"Perhaps they're having lunch before they leave."

"Don't even think about it!" I was very serious.

"Roger and out, General," she said.

Roger? – Oh, yeah …

Should I ring Karen? I didn't want to worry her. I'll phone her later, I thought. That was my big mistake.

Lower and lower came the clouds. The tops of the higher Tors were slowly disappearing into the white mist. The rocks of the Tor above me were still clear, but I knew that it was only a matter of time.

It was a quarter to one when the top of King's Tor disappeared into the clouds and there was still no sign of the tanker. I rang Bonzo's mobile.

"The mist is still coming down, and there's no sign of the damn tanker."

"Do you want to abort, General?"

"What? – Oh, yes – I mean 'no'. Even if I can't see the tanker when it leaves, you'll certainly see it – or hear it if the mist gets really bad – when it comes down the Merrivale road. Stay at your posts! And good luck! I'm going down to find Karen. I won't be able to see anything from up here in a couple of minutes … Hello? … Can you hear me?"

But Bonzo was no longer on the phone.

I dialled Karen's number. Nothing happened. Then, with horror, I realized what was happening. The display on my mobile told me: NO SIGNAL. I had lost contact with the outside world. And the mist was only inches above my head.

I grabbed Bonzo's mountain bike and shot off down the hillside towards the Dartmoor Way while I could still see it below me, a long ribbon of white. I would race down it to Routrundle Farm and meet Karen at the other end of the lane.

Or I thought I would, because everything turned out differently.

Chapter 16   Karen's adventure ♣

I hid Snuggles in some trees, sat down on a rock by the track leading to Routrundle Farm and waited.

It was very lonely out there on the moor and I was feeling fed up.

5   Why had I agreed to be posted out here where I would miss all the fun? It hadn't seemed a bad idea at the time – I would be at the most important post, Bonzo had said. But all he had wanted was to save all the adventure for himself and his girlfriend. Yes: girlfriend!

10   They must have thought that I was blind! I had seen them holding hands when they thought that nobody was looking on our trip to Plymouth the day before.

Selfish sex-mad pigs!

My mobile rang. It was General Ken.

15   "The red tanker's arrived and is filling up now. Are you ready down there?"

"Yes, General. We're ready."

"We?"

"Snuggles and me, Dumbo!"

20   Perhaps I shouldn't have called him Dumbo. Ken's really rather sweet, but how could he forget about Snuggles? I looked over at the trees where I had left him and walked over to join him. He snuggled up to me as usual, and I gave him a piece of sugar. I know it's bad for him, but I thought

25   he deserved a special treat.

It wasn't raining, but it seemed to be getting darker. When I looked up at the sky I realized why. The clouds were much lower. Only a little higher than the tops of the Tors. I thought about our poor General up there on his own. What would he think about our Dartmoor mists? Perhaps I should phone him and ask him if he can see anything, I thought, but just as I was about to dial his number, my mobile rang.

It was Bonzo. He sounded worried.

5   "We've lost contact with the General," he said. "It's the mist. It's on the Merrivale road now, but it's not too thick. Are you OK down there?"

"Yes, we're fine."

"We?"

10   "Snuggles and me." I didn't want to call him 'Dumbo', so I just *thought* the word to myself. "Any sign of the tanker?"

"Not yet. We're not even sure if it's left the laboratory yet."

So that was the situation. No contact with General Ken.
15 Mist coming down everywhere. No idea which way the red tanker would go or had already gone.

So much for Brother Bonzo's fine plan. I looked at my watch. The time had passed quickly. It was one o'clock already.

20   It was then that I heard it. The low sound of a diesel engine coming slowly up the hill towards me from Ward Bridge. So they had taken the Horrabridge road, and I would be at the most important post after all! I pushed Snuggles further back into the trees and waited. The sound of the engine came
25 nearer and, through the mist, I could see headlights. Closer and closer it came until at last I could see the silhouette of a truck – a tanker truck – a large red tanker truck.

It slowed down when it reached the right turn to Routrundle Farm, then turned right, past one of George
30 Weldon's nice new warning signs, and drove slowly up the track.

I took out my mobile and pointed it in their direction. The truck was about fifteen metres away and the mist was lifting a bit. I hoped they would not see the flash as I took the photo.

5   "Come on, Snuggles," I said. "Let's follow them!"

I was going to have my adventure after all.

Chapter 17   Helping hands ♠

It was one o'clock when I decided to phone Dad at the lab.
The mist was quite thick even down on the Merrivale road,
and now that I had lost contact with Ken there was no other
way of finding out which way the tanker had gone. We
5 couldn't wait any longer. I told Laney what I was going to
do, and she agreed.

Luckily, Dad was not busy, so he picked up the phone at
once.

"Where are you, son?" he asked even before I could say
10 anything.

"About a mile down the road from Princetown to
Merrivale. But listen, Dad, this is important. Which way did
the tanker go when it left the lab?"

"Towards Horrabridge, and George Weldon is following it.
15 Don't worry. I'm coming to get you and Laney right now."

"But how did you find out about our plan?" I asked
almost angrily.

"You didn't want to leave us out of your little adventure,
did you?"

20 Ten minutes later I was sitting in Dad's big Range Rover. I
had told Laney that we would pick her up and follow George
to wherever the tanker had gone.

It was a pity about Ken and Karen. They would be very
angry with us when they found out that we had left them
25 out of our big adventure. But they were only kids after all,
and there might be danger ahead.

*

When Uncle David and Bonzo picked me up, I was quite excited. I didn't really mind that the grown-ups had joined in our adventure because they can be quite useful. Stories about sixteen-year-olds who catch bank
5 robbers or other criminals all on their own don't happen in real life. You only read about them in books. This was *real*.

"Can you phone George and ask him where he is?" Uncle David asked Bonzo as we were driving through Princetown with our bikes in the back of the car. "And you, Laney, can
10 ring Ken and Karen and find out where *they* are."

I tried Ken's number – he could contact Karen even if I couldn't because of my stupid Teeny Text Tariff, of course – but I couldn't reach him. I hoped that nothing had gone wrong.

15 Bonzo was luckier. "Hello? George? Where are you?" Then he said nothing. He was listening. George was giving him instructions.

"George says he's followed the tanker up as far as the lane to Routrundle Farm. George has had to stop to answer
20 his mobile, of course. He wants us to go up the track from the Horrabridge road towards Routrundle. Then we've got them. He'll be at the other end. All we have to do is wait for the police. They're on their way. But he says that there was no sign of Karen at the end of the lane."

25 "Right," said Uncle David as he turned right onto the narrow track to Routrundle Farm. We'll drive up as far as Farmer Dawson's gate and wait there. He doesn't like people on his land."

"What about the red tanker truck, then?" I asked. "Isn't
30 that on his land?"

"Probably – but what on earth's that? Everybody out of the car and out of the way! Quick!"

Racing towards us down the narrow lane was a big red tanker.

And it didn't look as if it was going to stop at the gate.

*

Thank God for Bonzo's mountain bike, I thought as I raced down the hillside towards the Dartmoor Way.

Things really were beginning to move fast now. I had to be careful not to hit any rocks, of course, but I'm pretty good on a mountain bike even if I say so myself. And of course I kept a sharp lookout for bright green patches of ground which might be bogs. The Great Grimpen Mire …

But I was safely on the flat path now. The tops of the Tors were covered in mist, but it wasn't getting any lower. Should I stop and phone the others? At least tell Karen I was coming to meet her? Or should I look at the map to make sure where I was and where I wanted to go?

Bonzo had given us all a tourist brochure of the Dartmoor Way and there was quite a good map in it. Ahead of me was the tunnel where we had found the first traces of pollution the week before. I stopped and looked at the map. The path left the old railway track about half a mile after the tunnel and met the lane to Routrundle Farm, where Karen would be waiting with Snuggles.

I remembered that Routrundle was where Mr Dawson lived – Bonzo had called him a nutter, but I expect this was just his Australian way of saying that old Dawson didn't like strangers. Routrundle Farm would be around the corner of the next hill, near a stream which ran into the River Walkham.

A stream …

And Dawson didn't like strangers on his land. Was there a reason?

I cycled on through the dark tunnel, over the bridge and down the track until I could see the lane to the farm. There it was. I stopped the bike in shock. I had expected to see Karen and Snuggles at their post. Instead there was an old green Land Rover with the driver sitting in it. It looked as if he was making a call on his mobile. As I watched, the Land Rover began moving up the track. But where were Karen and Snuggles?

I cycled on, but suddenly I heard something which nearly made me fall off my bike. A loud cry for help – a cry which froze my blood, as they say – came from somewhere behind me, over my left shoulder. I turned round and saw four things on the track to the farm:

1   A big red tanker which suddenly drove off.
2   George Weldon getting out of his Land Rover.
3   Karen and Snuggles on the track behind it.
4   A man who had walked off the track and was now floundering up to his waist in the thick black mud of a bright green patch of bog.

If the description of the sudden death of a Dartmoor pony in the Great Grimpen Mire ('The Hound of the Baskervilles') was correct, the man had probably just over ninety seconds to live.

Chapter 18   Snuggles to the rescue

I got on Snuggles's back and slowly followed the tanker up the track towards Routrundle Farm. I didn't want the men to see me, of course. They might have caught me and taken my mobile off me – and as far as I knew I was the only one who had any evidence so far: a photo of the tanker going up a road which was closed to heavy trucks.

Stupid me! I took my mobile out of my pocket, picked Bonzo's number, and sent him a copy of the photo. How surprised he would be!

The track up to the farm was quite straight and I could see the tanker well. It was driving past the farm now, about half a mile away. Then the track sloped downwards towards the main road and I couldn't see the tanker any more. So they couldn't see me, could they? I would ride as far as the farm and see what I could see. I just hoped that the farmer – what had Bonzo called him? A nutter? – wouldn't come out and chase us away. But on Snuggles's back I felt over six feet tall, which is much taller than Bonzo or Laney or Ken.

"Come on, Snuggles! Trot!" I said, and we moved off at a quick trot.

The farmhouse looked empty as I passed it. Nobody at home, perhaps. I could see down into the valley now – and there was the tanker. Two men had got out of it and one of them was unrolling a long hose from the back of the truck.

I pulled out my mobile and took a couple of quick photos. I could see what they were going to do. They were going to pump what was in the tanker into a little stream near the farm!

I switched the phone function on and rang George Weldon's number.

"Hello?" said his voice.

"Where are you, Mr Weldon?" I never called him George when I was speaking to him.

"I'm following you up the track, young lady. What can you see?"

"They're pumping something out of the tanker into the stream below the farm! Hurry, or they'll get away!"

"Don't worry. Your dad and the others are at the other end of the track and the police are on their way here. They won't get away from us now."

I could hear his Land Rover quietly climbing the hill behind me.

Well, quietly – but not quietly enough. It's not a very quiet vehicle. One of the men looked up and saw me. At the same moment George's Land Rover came slowly past me and then accelerated down the hill towards the tanker. The driver jumped back into the driving seat and the man with the big hose dropped it and suddenly threw his arms into the air with a loud cry.

What was the matter with him? Why didn't he get back into the tanker?

Then he began to scream even louder: "Help! I'm sinking in the bog! Get me out! I can't move! Help me!"

My blood froze – as they say in horror stories, because this was a real horror story.

He had wanted to get back to the tanker so quickly that he had slipped and fallen into a bog! After two days of heavy rain this was no joke. George had got out of his Land Rover and was looking for something in the back.

The tanker had raced off down the lane with the long hose still bouncing about on the track behind it. I hoped the driver had gone off to look for help, but I couldn't be sure. It takes about a minute and a half for somebody to sink into a deep bog – maybe a little more if he doesn't struggle.

"Hurry!" the man screamed again. "Please hurry! I'm sinking!"

And he was. He was floundering up to his waist in the thick black mud – mud that had no solid ground at the bottom.

I rode quickly down to the Land Rover and jumped off Snuggles.

George had at last found a long rope in the back of the Land Rover.

"Stand still and don't struggle!" he shouted to the man. "We'll get you out." He threw the rope across to the middle of the bog and the man caught it. "Tie the rope under your arms and hold on to it!"

George and I both pulled as hard as we could, but it was no use. The man was still sinking. The mud was up to his shoulders, and he was screaming desperately. It was then that I had my best idea ever.

"Snuggles! Come here!"

We tied our end of the rope to Snuggles's saddle and, slowly but surely, pulled the man to the side of the track. When we got him out at last, he just lay there on the grass until the police arrived a few minutes later.

I took out my mobile and took one photo after the other – until the battery was empty.

Ken had seen everything from the other side of the valley. He was standing a long way away, but I took a photo of him anyway. He was jumping up and down like a loony. I

couldn't tell whether he was happy or angry with me. Later
on, he told me he had been jumping for joy.

My last photo was of Dad, Bonzo and Laney coming up
the track towards me followed by two policemen. The tanker
driver was walking between them.

....

We all got our photos in the newspapers, of course. But Karen was the winner. A newspaper paid her £250 for the photos she had taken with her mobile. She said she would share the money with us. Good old Karen!

5   At first we were all a bit angry at George Weldon for telling Dad all about our wonderful plan to catch the polluters, but when he told us that he hadn't wanted to spoil our fun, we all felt a bit better.

After all, stories where teenagers manage to beat the 10 Mafia or bust drug rings or catch bank robbers without any help from grown-ups are just stories.

Laney and Ken will be staying with us until the end of the holidays, but I can't think of anything else that we could do after this first week!

*

15   Mum was shocked, of course. But she's coming out of hospital next week and will be coming down to Devon as soon as she can – to look after me and Ken, she says.

I think she's just disappointed that she didn't have 20 adventures like ours when she was a girl.

Of course we appreciated the help we got from the grown-ups, and the best news of all was when Uncle David told us that the 'special waste' which the tanker had taken away with the enigmatic XX 49 chalked on its side was a special 25 preparation of salt water which could do very little damage to the environment.

ls, but the
claim over
st one
shion.
Lahore, the
d, wearing
well below the
ers, unlike her
g of an outcry
ue in 1991.

(photo: M. Fleis

Britain

ng again

Pollution Busters!

(Tavistock) Four teenage pollution busters,
of pony Snuggles, helped to stop
s and rivers in Dartmo
Karen li

Good old Uncle David! I'm sure that, at the beginning,
Bonzo thought that his dad was somehow mixed up in this
pollution business. I'm glad he wasn't, because I like him
– and his son – very much.

*

I only wish I had been a bit closer to the action. I cycled down to the lane and back up the track to the farm, but by then it was all over.

I really was jumping for joy when I saw Karen and
5 Snuggles pull the man out of the bog. The driver, by the way, was old Farmer Dawson himself. No wonder he didn't like strangers on his land: he was allowing his son-in-law – the fool who fell into the bog – to dump chemical waste in the streams near his farm.

10 The owner of ENVIRONMENTAL PROCESSORS (TAVI-STOCK) Ltd, was an old friend of Dawson's, and all three shared the money for waste disposal from XX 49. I expect all three will find a new home for a few years in nearby Princetown.

15 I'm looking forward to my first riding lesson on Snuggles tomorrow. I was wrong about girls with ponies. But that's still my little secret.

*

Dear Snuggles! What would we have done without you? Even Ken has, I think, changed his mind about
20 you – and about me, perhaps. I know he thinks I don't know that he quite likes me now – but boys are not very good about keeping secrets like that!

If I do nothing else this holidays, I'm going to teach Ken to ride. Laney seems to be more interested in boys than
25 ponies, so I don't suppose she'll have much time for riding.

How silly it was of Bonzo and me to be disappointed when we discovered that we had been looking forward to a boy or, in my case, a girl of the same age.

I like Ken. It was sweet of him to lie about the moor pony
30 in 'The Hound of the Baskervilles' when he told me that

Sherlock Holmes and Dr Watson had pulled it out of the Great Grimpen Mire. He just wanted to spare my feelings. I knew all the time that the pony had sunk to the bottom and died because although I haven't read the book, I saw the film 5 on TV years ago.

Girls are not as sensitive as some boys think – at least this girl isn't!

Vocabulary

A

Aborigine [ˌæbəˈrɪdʒəni]
Ureinwohner Australiens
(to) **abort** [əˈbɔːt] vorzeitig
abbrechen
(to) **accelerate** beschleunigen
adult [ˈædʌlt] Erwachsene/r
advert [ˈædvɜːt] Anzeige
(to) **appreciate** schätzen; zu
schätzen wissen
(to) **argue** sich streiten
argument *hier:* Streit
arrival Ankunft
astonished erstaunt
attention Aufmerksamkeit
Aye-aye *bei der Marine:* Zu
Befehl!

B

(to) **back** rückwärts fahren
backwards rückwärts
(to) **bake** backen
(to) **behave oneself**
sich benehmen
bend Kurve
binoculars [bɪˈnɒkjələz]
Feldstecher
bog Sumpf; Morast
bored gelangweilt
bossy rechthaberisch;
herrschsüchtig
bother Ärger, Kummer
(to) **bother** sich Mühe geben
(to) **bounce** aufprallen
(wie ein Ball)

brake Bremse
branch Ast
Brit *slang:* Brite, Britin
(to) **burst – burst**
– burst platzen; **to burst**
out laughing = in heftiges
Gelächter ausbrechen
(to) **bust** zum Platzen bringen;
auffliegen lassen
(to) **buzz** sb. jdn. anrufen

C

cab Fahrerhaus
campaign Kampagne
car-sick reisekrank
catastrophe [kəˈtæstrəfi]
Katastrophe
(to) **chalk** mit Kreide
(auf)schreiben
cheek Wange; Backe
chemical chemisch; Chemikalie
chemist Chemiker
chin Kinn
(to) **clear off** abhauen
close dicht
cloud Wolke
(to) **comment** bemerken
condition Bedingung
confused durcheinander
confusion Verwirrung;
Durcheinander
connection Verbindung
convict [ˈkɒnvɪkt] *altmodisch:*
Zuchthäusler
(to) **convince** überzeugen

corporal Obergefreite/r
countryside Landschaft
Countryside Warden
  Landschaftswart
  (im Nationalpark usw.)
cream Sahne
criminal Verbrecher/in
curly kraus
cynical zynisch

D

daft bat *slang:* blöde Schnalle
  (bat = Fledermaus)
damn verdammt
deadly tödlich; tot-
Big deal! *ironisch:* Wunderbar!
  Wie toll!
defensive defensiv
delay Verzögerung; *im Stau:*
  Wartezeit
delicious köstlich
(to) **deliver** liefern
depressing deprimierend
(to) **deserve** verdienen
desperate ['despərət] verzweifelt
dessert [dɪ'zɜːt] Dessert
(to) **dial** wählen
  (Telefonnummer)
disappointed enttäuscht
disinfectant
  Desinfektionsmittel
disposal Entsorgung
distinct deutlich
(to) **distract** ablenken
(to) **disturb** stören
(to be) doubled up sich
  krümmen (vor Lachen usw.)
downhill bergab
downwards abwärts

dozen Dutzend
(to) **drag** schleppen
drain Abflussrinne, -rohr
dramatic dramatisch
(to) **drip** tropfen
driving licence Führerschein
Dumbo *slang:* blöde Person
dump Ort: Loch
(to) **dump** abladen; (Müll)
  kippen

E

earplug Ohrstöpsel
embarrassing peinlich
especially besonders; speziell
evidence Beweismittel
exception Ausnahme
excitement Aufregung
(to) **expect** erwarten;
  annehmen
explorer Entdecker; Forscher

F

farmer Bauer; Landwirt
farmyard Bauernhof
fence Zaun
fertilizer Düngemittel
field marshal Feldmarschall
flash Blitz; Aufblitzen
flat flach
(to) **float** schwimmen
  (= treiben)
(to) **flounder** umherstolpern
(to) **flow** fließen
fool Idiot; Dummkopf
forecast Vorhersage
four-wheel-drive vehicle
  ['viːəkl] Fahrzeug mit
  Allradantrieb

freckles Sommersprossen

(to) **freeze – froze – frozen** gefrieren

(to) **frown** die Stirn runzeln

f-word ordinäres Schimpfwort, das mit f- anfängt

G

gas-guzzler Benzinschlucker

geek Kauz; komischer Typ

geeky-looking komisch aussehend

(to) **get going** sich auf den Weg machen

Get off! hier, *als Ausruf:* Lass los!

ghostly geisterhaft

(to) **give sb. a hand** jdn. helfen

(to) **go fishing** Angeln gehen

(to) **grab** schnell (an)packen

grass Gras

grown-up Erwachsene/r

(to) **guarantee** garantieren

guess *hier:* Ratemöglichkeit

H

halfway auf halbem Weg; halbwegs

(to) **hand** aushändigen

headlight Scheinwerfer

hell Hölle; Who the hell? = Wer in aller Welt?

helpful hilfreich

second helping Nachschlag

(to) **hide – hid – hidden** verstecken

Highways Department Straßenbauamt

hillside Hang; Seite eines Hügels

honest ehrlich

horizon Horizont

hose Schlauch

hound (Jagd-) Hund

huge riesig; gewaltig

humour Humor

(to) **hurry** sich beeilen

I

(to) **ignore** nicht beachten

impatient ungeduldig

impossible unmöglich

inch engl. Maßeinheit: Zoll; 2,45 cm

indeed in der Tat

industrial [ɪn'dʌstrɪəl] Industrie-; industriell

industrial estate Industriegebiet

instead stattdessen

instead of anstatt

intelligence Intelligenz

interest Interesse

(to) **interrupt** unterbrechen

(to) **introduce oneself** sich vorstellen

Iron Age ['aɪəneɪdʒ] Eisenzeit

J

joke Witz

joy Freude

junction Einmündung; Kreuzung

K

(to be) **keen on** sth. auf etwas scharf sein

key Schlüssel

(to) **kiss** küssen

L

laboratory [lə'bɒrətri] Labor
  (*abgekürzt:* **lab** [læb])
lamb chop [læm'tʃɒp]
  Lammkotelett
landscape Landschaft
lane Gasse; schmale Landstraße
laughter Gelächter; Lachen
at least wenigstens
(to) **let go** los lassen
level eben
lid Deckel
(to) **lie** lügen
likely wahrscheinlich
liquid flüssig; Flüssigkeit
logic-free logikfrei; nicht logisch
  zusammenhängend
(to keep a) lookout Ausschau
  (halten)
loony Verrückte/r
low niedrig

M

(to) **manage** schaffen
marvellous wunderbar; herrlich
(to) **mention** erwähnen
Midsummer's Day
  die Sommersonnenwende
  (21. Juni)
I don't mind es macht mir nichts
  aus
minimization Minimierung
minus Minus-; minus
mire Morast; Sumpf
misunderstanding
  Missverständnis
moor Hoch-, Heidemoor
moorland Moor-,
  Heidelandschaft

N

nasty hässlich
naughty unartig
navy Kriegsmarine
nearby nahe gelegen
neighbourhood Nachbarschaft
What a nerve! Der hat Nerven!
  Wie frech!
northwards nordwärts; in
  Richtung Norden
nowadays heutzutage
nutter Verrückte/r

O

official amtlich
old-fashioned altmodisch
opening Öffnung
ordinary gewöhnlich; normal
otter Fischotter
(to) **overlook** übersehen
on one's own allein
owner Besitzer

P

packhorse Lastpferd;
  Saumpferd
paedophile Pädophiler;
  Kinderschänder
paradise Paradies
passage Gang; Passage
(to) **pat** leicht klopfen
patch *hier:* Flecken
patient geduldig
pause (Sprech-) Pause
petrol Benzin
pile Stapel
(to) **pile into** schnell einsteigen
pipe Rohr

it's a pity es ist schade
poison Gift
(to) **poison** vergiften
polite höflich
pollutant [pə'luːtənt]
　umweltverschmutzender
　Stoff
pool Tümpel; Weiher
prehistoric vorgeschichtlich
prejudiced ['predʒədɪst]
　voreingenommen
preparation Aufbereitung;
　Vorbereitung
(to) **pretend** so tun, als ob
pretty *hier:* ziemlich
probably wahrscheinlich
(to) **prohibit** [prə'hɪbɪt]
　verbieten
proof Beweis(e)
proper richtig
psychological [ˌsaɪkə'lɒdʒɪkl]
　psychologisch
(to) **pump** pumpen
(to) **punish** bestrafen

Q

quarry Steinbruch

R

(to) **race** jagen; rennen
rat Ratte
rear mirror Rückspiegel
(to) **catch sb. red-handed** jdn.
　auf frischer Tat ertappen
relative Verwandte/r
rescue Rettung
respect Respekt
responsibility Verantwortung
ribbon Band

(to) **get rid of sth.** etwas
　loswerden
robber Räuber
Roger and out Funkersprache:
　Ende!
to roll rollen; sich wälzen
rolling hills sanfte Hügel
roof Dach; *hier:* Tunneldecke
rubber boot Gummistiefel

S

saddle Sattel
saddlebag Satteltasche
salt [sɔːlt] Salz
sample Probe
scenery Landschaft
scientist
　Naturwissenschaftler/in
scones [skɒnz] kleine runde
　Brötchen, die mit Backpulver
　gebacken werden
secret Geheimnis
top secret streng geheim
(to) **select** aussuchen
selfish selbstsüchtig
sensitive empfindlich
separate getrennt
serviette [ˌsɜːvi'et] Serviette
shade (Farb-) Schattierung
(to) **share** teilen
short cut Wegkürzung
(to be) **sick** sich übergeben
(to feel) **sick** Übelkeit
　verspüren; sich unwohl
　fühlen
(to) **sign** unterschreiben
silence Schweigen; Stille
silhouette [ˌsɪlu'et] Silhouette
slight leicht

slippery rutschig

(to) **slope** abfallen

slowcoach eine trödlige Person

(to) **slow down** (sich)
verlangsamen; langsamer
fahren

smell Geruch

(to) **snuggle** kuscheln

solid fest

son-in-law Schwiegersohn

source Quelle

(to) **spare** schonen

(to) **split up** *hier:* sich verteilen

(to) **spoil** verderben

spooky gespenstisch

(to) **squash** quetschen

(to) **squeak** quietschen

stable Pferdestall

(to) **stare** starren

star-shaped sternförmig

steep steil

(to) **stick out** herausragen;
hervorstechen

strawberry Erdbeere

stream Bach

(to) **struggle** Widerstand leisten

sugar ['ʃʊgə] Zucker

sunlight Sonnenlicht

sunshine Sonnenschein

(to) **suspect** [sə'spekt]
verdächtigen

suspicious argwöhnisch;
verdächtig

(to) **swallow** (ver)schlucken

Sweetie *Anrede:* Süße

(to) **switch on** anschalten

What a swiz! *altmodisch:* Welch
ein Schwindel/Betrug!

symbol Symbol; Sinnbild

T

tactful taktvoll

tanker Tankwagen

(to) **tap out** (etwas unbeholfen)
tippen; rhythmisch klopfen

tariff ['tærɪf] Tarif; Kostenplan

task Aufgabe

(to) **taste** schmecken

thoughtful nachdenklich

threat Drohung

townie abschätzig: Stadtpflanze

trace Spur; Anzeichen

track Fährte; Eisenbahntrasse

on track im Plan; im grünen
Bereich

trainers Turnschuhe;
Sportschuhe

trap Falle

treat Hochgenuss

triumph Triumph

(to) **trot** traben;
at the trot = im Trab

truck Lastwagen

tunnel Tunnel

typical typisch

tyre Reifen

U

underground unterirdisch

unless es sei denn

(to) **unroll** ausrollen

unusual ungewöhnlich

uphill bergauf

V

vague [veɪg] vage

vehicle ['viːəkl] Fahrzeug

W

waist Taille

wander (ziellos hin und her) wandern

waste Abfall; Müll

waste disposal Abfallentsorgung

(to be) on watch auf der Hut sein

(to) **wave** winken

weirdo ['wɪədəʊ] Sonderling; seltsamer Mensch

wheel Rad

wimp Schwächling

(to) **wipe** wischen

wire Draht

Y

yackety-yackety-yak Lautmalerei: endloses Geschwätz

yeah *slang:* yes

Questions and Activities

....

Before you start

Find a map of Dartmoor on the Internet (*multimap.com* is a useful website) and print out a version which shows the countryside between Tavistock and Princetown (the best scale to choose is 1:25,000 = 2.5 centimetres to the kilometre). Then you can follow the adventure in detail. You will not find High Tor or High Tor House on the map because these are not names of real places, but you will find Horrabridge, the River Walkham, the Dartmoor Way and most of the other places in the story.

Go to the Internet and type "Dartmoor". Choose a tourist website and find some good photos of the area.

You may also like to watch a video or DVD of *The Hound of the Baskervilles* (there are several – including a cartoon version). This will give you an idea of the Dartmoor countryside.

Chapter 1 – Laney introduces herself

Without reading the chapter again, write down a few sentences about Laney. Describe her and say something about her family background, the things she likes and dislikes etc. If you like, you can read the first chapter again to make sure that you have not left anything important out. Then answer the questions below.

Questions for girls:

1   Would you say that you have the same likes and dislikes as Laney?

2   In what ways is Laney like you – or unlike you?

3 Do you have a mobile? What do you use it for?

4 What do you know about Laney's family situation?

5 What does Laney think about her younger brother Ken?

Questions for boys:

1 Would you say that Laney is a typical 15-year-old? Give reasons for your opinion.

2 In what ways is Ken like you – or unlike you?

3 Do you have a mobile? What do you use it for?

4 Do you think that Ken has problems with his sister? Give your reasons.

5 Would you describe Ken as 'cool'? Give your reasons.

Chapter 2 – Ken introduces himself

1 Do you agree with Ken's opinion of his older sister Laney? Compare your reasons with those of a girl in your class, if you are a boy, or with a boy in your class, if you are a girl. Do you both agree?

2 What sort of things do you like (or dislike) doing when you are on holiday?

3 Find one or two examples of Ken's sense of humour from this chapter.

4 Why does Ken say that he must be the most boring thirteen-year-old in the world? Do you agree with him, or is this another example of his sense of humour?

Chapter 3 – Bonzo introduces himself

1 Without reading this short chapter again, write as much as you can remember about Bonzo and his family.

2 Do you think Bonzo is older or younger than his sister Karen?

3 Do you think Bonzo enjoys living on the edge of Dartmoor? Give one or two reasons why or why not.

4 Have you ever been to London – or Adelaide? Find some material about these two cities and write a few sentences about each one. Which one would you rather live in?

5 Why do you think Bonzo prefers Adelaide to London?

6 Would you like to be a 'globetrotter' like Bonzo? Say why or why not.

Chapter 4 – Karen introduces herself

1 Do you agree with Bonzo that Karen is a wimp?

2 Do you agree with Karen that the youngest family member often does not get enough attention?

3 Do you think that Mrs Rawlinson (Bonzo's and Karen's mother) is a bad driver, or is Karen just a nervous little girl?

4 What sort of a car is a Range Rover? Find out on the Internet!

5 Why do you think that the Rawlinsons need a car like this?

Chapter 5 – Arrival and confusion

1 Why was Laney fed up when the train finally reached Plymouth?

2 In this chapter, which of the four children
a shows the best sense of humour? ....
b is most embarrassed by the situation? ....
c tries to save Laney from embarrassment? ....
d does absolutely nothing? ....

3 Explain in your own words how this confusing situation developed?

4 *Question for boys:*

Would you have embarrassed Laney if you had been Bonzo?

Question for girls:

How would you have reacted in such an embarrassing situation?

Chapter 6 – High Tor House

1 Why is Ken so disappointed at the start of this chapter?

2 Is Ken still disappointed at the end of the chapter? Say why or why not.

3 Where would you put Ken's politeness on a scale from 1 *(sehr gut)* to 6 *(mangelhaft)*. Give your reasons.

4 Find another example of Bonzo's sense of humour in this chapter. Explain why what he says is so funny.

Chapter 7 – Slowly making friends

1 This chapter is written from the viewpoints of each of the four children. They explain how they are getting over their disappointments. Say why they are disappointed and how they get over their disappointments?

2 Do all four children get over their disappointments?

3 Is there anyone you feel sorry for in this chapter?

Chapter 8 – A walk to King's Tor

Here are ten definitions of words in this chapter. Find the words that go with the definitions:

1 You can see a long way with these:

    ....

2 Place where bad people are put:

    ....

3 Feeling that a person is as good as or better than you:

....

4 Place where the ground is very soft and wet:

....

5 Person who finds out facts about an unknown country:

....

6 Animal which can carry heavy things:

....

7 Small animal which lives in water and eats fish:

....

8 Line between the land or sea and the sky:

....

9 This is wider than a track but narrower than a road:

....

10 People often eat these for breakfast in Britain:

....

Chapter 9 – A shock for Karen

1 Is Karen disappointed because she cannot go on with the others? Say why or why not.

2 Why is Karen surprised to see a truck in the lane?

3 Why isn't Karen afraid of the two men?

4 Why does Karen watch what the men do next?

5 What does an orange plate on the back of a truck mean?

6 What do you think the letters XX 49 mean?

Chapter 10 – George Weldon is worried

1 Write a few sentences about the job of a Countryside Warden in Britain. For more information, look up "Countryside Warden" on the Internet.

2 Laney thinks that Bonzo knows something which he doesn't want the others to know. What could this secret be?

3 What do you think is happening in this quiet corner of the Dartmoor National Park?

4 Do you think there is a connection between what the three young people have found out in this chapter and Karen's 'adventure' in Chapter 9? What could it be?

Chapter 11 – Ken and Karen put two and two together

1 Has your opinion about shy little Karen changed a little? Explain this change.

2 Do you think that Bonzo's father has anything to do with the pollution?

3 English idioms Do you know the meaning of 'to put two and two together'? Look at the idiomatic phrases below and match them to their definitions:

to put two and two together	to come to the wrong conclusion
a dark horse	an intelligent person
to hit the nail on the head	to come to a conclusion which may or may not be correct.
a bright spark	a person with unsuspected qualities
to be barking up the wrong tree	to come to a correct conclusion

Chapter 12 – Uncle David

1   Do you believe that Uncle David could be connected with the pollution of the rivers and streams? Give your reasons.

2   What sort of work do you think is going on at the secret laboratory?

3   Why does Uncle David get angry when they start talking about pollution?

4   Explain the way in which Laney 'handles' Uncle David when she asks him about pollution. Would Bonzo or Ken have got the same results?

5   We do not know much about Aunt Megan so far, but she makes a big contribution towards Laney's successful 'interview' with her husband. What is it?

Chapter 13 – A trip to Tavistock

1   Have a look on the Internet for tourist information about Tavistock.

2   Would you like to visit Tavistock and Dartmoor? Give reasons why or why not.

3   Who has the best idea in this chapter?

4   Could you have thought of a better plan? What would you have done?

5   Why does Karen hide?

6   This is Chapter 13! The numbers on the truck registration plate add up to 13. Do you think that 13 is an unlucky number? Where does this idea come from? If you know the answer, write it down. If you don't, surf the Net (*wikipedia.com* is a good starting point).

Chapter 14 – Working out the plan

1 Dartmoor Prison was built for French prisoners-of-war during the Napoleonic Wars, which ended in 1815. Find out about it on the Internet.

2 If you have printed out a map of the area, check the routes taken by Laney/Bonzo and Ken/Karen. Do you think they have missed any possible dumping places? Put a red cross on any places which they may have missed.

3 The four young people have found seven or eight dumping places. Mark the places on your map with a green cross.

4 Why does Bonzo smile when Laney says: "We will have to be patient"?

5 Do you think the new road signs will solve the problem? Say why or why not.

6 Why do you think that George Weldon looks at the four young people 'as if he couldn't quite believe' them at the end of the chapter?

Chapter 15 – General Ken

1 Is Ken happy with his part in the plan at the beginning of the chapter? Say why or why not.

2 Who is more important in the army: a corporal, a general or a field marshal?

3 Find some examples of Bonzo's tact in this chapter.

4 Find some examples of 'military' language in this chapter.

Chapter 16 – Karen's adventure

1 Why is Karen angry about Laney and Bonzo's behaviour in Plymouth?

2 Karen is fed up at the beginning of the chapter. What feelings does she have at the end?

3 What ironical aspect of Bonzo's plan becomes clear during this chapter?

4 Using the situations in Chapters 15 and 16, write a short telephone conversation between Bonzo and Laney about the problems of the situation.

Chapter 17 – Helping hands

1 Why is Bonzo angry?

2 Is Bonzo right when he thinks that Ken and Karen have been left out of the adventure?

3 Why can't Laney ring Karen on her mobile?

4 Why do they suddenly jump out of the Range Rover on their way to Routrundle Farm?

5 Ken thinks that there is a connection between Mr Dawson and the polluters. Why does he think so?

6 This chapter ends dramatically. What do you think will happen in the next chapter? Write a few ideas down.

7 What has Karen been doing in the time between Chapter 16 and the moment Ken sees her? Write the continuation of 'Karen's adventure' from her viewpoint. You can compare it with the next chapter.

Chapter 18 – Snuggles to the rescue

1 This is a chapter for pony-lovers. Did you enjoy it? Say why or why not.

2 Do you think that the truck driver drove off to get help?

3 George Weldon is a fine Countryside Warden, but not a quick thinker. What more could he have done to pull the man out of the bog?

4 What has happened between the time when the tanker came racing down the hill from Routrundle Farm in the last chapter and the moment that Karen sees the others walking up the lane? Write the story from the viewpoint of Bonzo *(if you are a boy)* or Laney *(if you are a girl)*.

Chapter 19 – All's well that ends well

1 Anticlimax! Have you any ideas about what the young people could do for the rest of the holidays?

2 What is the best piece of news in this final chapter?

3 What do you think will happen to the three polluters?

4 Give your reasons why you think the young people could or couldn't have handled the situation without the help of adults.

5 In what way do you think Ken has changed his mind about Karen?

6 Karen has the last word in the story. In what ways has your opinion of her changed since you first 'met' her in Chapter 3?

Project work

1 "We all got our photos in the newspapers, of course," says Bonzo at the end of the story. Write a newspaper article about the 'pollution busters'.

2 Each chapter of this story is written from the viewpoint of one of the young people, boy or girl. If you are a boy, you may not agree with the way a girl writes about one or both of the boys in the chapter, and vice versa.

Task for girls

Take a chapter written from the viewpoint of one of the boys and re-write it – or some of it – from the viewpoint of one of the girls.

Task for boys

Take a chapter written from the viewpoint of one of the girls and re-write it – or some of it – from the viewpoint of one of the boys.

The chapter which you select should not be too long and must contain at least one person of each sex. Do not change any of the actual dialogues.

3 Did you enjoy the story? Which character did you 'like' best? Talk about the story and the characters with your friends or classmates (if you read this story at school).

4 Are there any ways in which you personally could become a 'pollution buster'? Even always remembering to put your litter in a litter bin would be a good start. Talk about pollution problems with your friends or classmates.